The Prince of
A Trage

Thomas Godfrey
(Editor: Montrose Jonas Moses)

Alpha Editions

This edition published in 2024

ISBN 9789362090058

Design and Setting By

Alpha Editions
www.alphaedis.com

Email - info@alphaedis.com

Contents

THOMAS GODFREY, JR.

(1736-1763)

Thomas Godfrey, Jr., was born in Philadelphia, on December 4, 1736, the son of a man who himself won fame as an inventor of the Quadrant. Godfrey, Senior, was a friend of Benjamin Franklin, the two probably having been drawn together by their common interest in science. When Godfrey, Senior, died, December, 1749, it was Franklin who wrote his obituary notice.[1]

Young Godfrey was a student at the College or Academy of Philadelphia, and when his education was completed, he became apprenticed to a watch-maker, remaining in that profession until 1758. As a student at the Academy, he came under the special influence of Dr. William Smith, the first Principal or Provost of that institution,[2] and it was Dr. Smith who not only obtained for Godfrey a lieutenancy with the Pennsylvania troops in 1758, which sent him in the expedition against Fort Duquesne, but who, likewise, as the Editor of *The American Magazine*, was only too glad to accept and publish some of Godfrey's poetical effusions.

That the young man was popular, and that he associated with some of the most promising figures of the time, will be seen from the fact that, although he was only twenty-seven when he died, he was counted among the friends of Benjamin West and John Green, both portrait painters, of Francis Hopkinson, who was a student at the College of Philadelphia, and of Nathaniel Evans, a young minister whose loyalty found outlet after Godfrey's death in the Memorial Edition of Godfrey's works. Evans himself wrote poems and dialogues. In his confirmation of the fact that, as a poet, Godfrey was regarded favourably by the Philadelphians of the time, he quotes from the diaryof one Miss Sarah Eve, who referred to him as "our poet."

Godfrey's reputation, as a young man with musical talents and a decided taste for painting, has come down to us. Certain it is that, during all of this time of varied occupation as a watch-maker and a soldier, he must have been courting the poetic Muse. There are some who speculate, without authority, on his having been a theatre-goer, and having become inspired as a playwright by the work of the American Company, in Philadelphia; especially by the good work of Douglass. Because of insufficient evidence, that is a question which remains unproven. Nevertheless, it is certain, from an extant letter written by Godfrey on November 17, 1759, and quoted by

Seilhamer, that he must have had his attention turned to playwriting as a special art. He says to his correspondent, writing from North Carolina:

By the last vessel from this place, I sent you the copy of a tragedy I finished here, and desired your interest in bringing it on the stage; I have not yet heard of the vessel's safe arrival, and believe if she is safe it will be too late for the company now in Philadelphia. [Meaning, of course, Douglass's company.]

There are two facts to be noted in this communication: first, that it was written from North Carolina, where, in 1759, Godfrey had gone on some plantation business—probably as factor; and second, that it must have been penned with the idea of immediate production by the actors in Philadelphia. According to Seilhamer, Godfrey remained in North Carolina for three years. He did not write the entire manuscript of "The Prince of Parthia" while living in the South but, as he definitely states in his letter, finished it soon after his arrival.

There is no evidence as to why Godfrey sailed to the Island of New Providence in the last year of his life, and then returned to Wilmington, N.C. There is no definite statement as to whether he contracted fever and had a sunstroke on that expedition, or after his return home. But, nevertheless, he did contract the fever and have a sunstroke; with the result that he succumbed to his illness, and died near Wilmington, North Carolina, on August 3, 1763.[3]

After his death, Godfrey's friends decided among themselves that the young man was too much of a genius for them to allow his productions to remain scattered and unrecognized. Evidently, correspondence regarding this must have taken place between Dr. Smith, Nathaniel Evans, the young minister, and John Green, the portrait painter. For, in 1765, a book was published, entitled "Juvenile Poems on Various Subjects, with the Prince of Parthia," printed in Philadelphia by one Henry Miller.[4] The volume contained a life written by Evans, a critical estimate written by Dr. Smith, of the College of Philadelphia, and an Elegy from the pen of John Green, who had been previously complimented by Godfrey in a poem entitled "A Night Piece." The whole spirit of the publication was one of friendly devotion and of firm belief in the permanency of Godfrey's position in the literary world. As was the custom of the time, the Edition was issued under the patronage of subscribers, a list being included. We know, for example, that Benjamin Franklin subscribed for twelve copies, his own private, autographed copy having been put on sale a few years ago.

As yet, no concerted effort had been made for the production of Godfrey's "The Prince of Parthia." We do not know if, during this time, the American Company had any claim on the manuscript, or whether, after Godfrey's death, it was again submitted to the theatrical people. But this much we do know, that, very hastily, the American Company, headed by David Douglass, who was playing at the Southwark Theatre in Philadelphia, decided that they would put on "The Prince of Parthia" in place of "The Disappointment; or, the Force of Credulity," a comic opera which will be noted in my introduction to John Leacock's "The Fall of British Tyranny." This musical piece had actually been put into rehearsal in 1767, when it was withdrawn. Immediately, the *Pennsylvania Journal and Weekly Advertiser* for April 23, 1767, contained an advertisement of the forthcoming production; it ran as follows:

By Authority./Never Performed before./By the American Company,/at the New Theatre, in Southwark,/On Friday, the Twenty-fourth of April, will be/presented, A Tragedy written by the late ingenious/Mr. *Thomas Godfrey*, of this city, called the/Prince of Parthia./The Principal Characters by Mr. Hallam,/Mr. Douglass, Mr. Wall, Mr. Morris,/Mr. Allyn, Mr. Tomlinson, Mr. Broad/belt, Mr. Greville, Mrs. Douglass,/Mrs. Morris, Miss Wainwight, and/Miss Cheer./To which will be added, A Ballad Opera called/The Contrivances./To begin exactly at *Seven o'clock.—Vivant Rex & Regina./*

In the *Pennsylvania Gazette*, for the same date, appears an advertisement, without the cast of characters.

The production occurred on April 24, 1767.

Seilhamer gives a probable cast of characters, although only the list of actors is given in the advertisement. Apart from this, little is known of the production: whether or not it pleased the theatre-goers of the time. We can judge, however, from the reading of the play itself, that there was little of extreme dramatic excellence in the situations, the chief claim, from the actor's point of view, being the opportunity to deliver certain very highly coloured, poetical lines modelled after the manner of the Elizabethan drama.

In the publication of "The Prince of Parthia," we have the first printed American tragedy in existence, and in its production we have one of only two plays, written by Americans, and presented on the stage before the Revolution. The other play is George Cockings's "The Conquest of Canada; or, The Siege of Quebec," printed for the author in 1766, and presented in Philadelphia in 1773. We note, in Dr. F. W. Atkinson's estimable Bibliography of American Plays in his possession, that Cockings later described himself as "Camillo Querno, Poet Laureate to Congress."

The interest in the early history of the American drama, which has become evident within recent years, and nowhere more evident than among the student body in our American colleges, induced the Zelosophic Literary Society, encouraged by the University of Pennsylvania, to revive "The Prince of Parthia," which was written by one of their alumni. The production was consummated on March 26, 1915. Even though we have no statement as to the actual manner in which the Douglass Company presented the play originally, we are given every evidence, by those who witnessed the revival, that the play, while containing many excellences, was not of a dramatic character according to modern ideas of stage effectiveness.

The only portrait of Godfrey known to have been in existence was that painted by Benjamin West, in his earlier years. It is interesting to note that in commemoration of the one hundred and fiftieth anniversary of the original production of this play, Dr. Archibald Henderson, of the University of North Carolina, issued an *édition de luxe* of "The Prince of Parthia," with an extended introduction, historical, biographical and critical (Boston: Little, Brown & Co., 1917).

FOOTNOTES:

[1] A notice appeared in the Pennsylvania *Gazette*, December 19, 1749. See Scharf and Westcott's "History of Philadelphia" for references to Godfrey, Sr. Therein is given a picture of his house in Germantown, Pa. Barlow mentions him in his "Columbiad." A monument to his memory was erected in Laurel Hill Cemetery, Philadelphia, 1843. Note that David Rittenhouse, an American dramatist who translated, from the German, "Lucy Sampson; or, The Unhappy Heiress" (1789), was likewise a mathematical genius.

[2] Accounts of Dr. Smith are to be found in Henry Simpson's "Eminent Philadelphians"; Scharf & Westcott's "History of Philadelphia," ii, 1126. Dr. Smith's "Life and Correspondence," by Horace Wemyss Smith, was issued in 2 vols., 1879.

[3] Visitors to Wilmington, N.C., will be taken to Old St. James's Church-yard, where Godfrey lies buried.

[4] Juvenile Poems/on/Various Subjects./With the/Prince of Parthia,/A/Tragedy,/By the Late/Mr. Thomas Godfrey, Junr./of Philadelphia./To which is prefixed,/Some Account of the Author and his Writings./Poeta nascitur non fit. Hor./Philadelphia,/Printed by Henry Miller, in Second-Street./M DCC LXV.

JUVENILE POEMS

ON

VARIOUS SUBJECTS.

WITH THE

PRINCE OF PARTHIA,

A

T R A G E D Y.

BY THE LATE

Mr. *THOMAS GODFREY*, Junr.

of PHILADELPHIA.

To which is prefixed,

Some ACCOUNT of the *AUTHOR* and his *WRITINGS*.

Poeta nascitur non fit. HOR.

PHILADELPHIA,

Printed by HENRY MILLER, in Second-Street.

M DCC LXV.

Fac-Simile of Original Title-Page to First Edition

ADVERTISEMENT

Our Author has made Use of the *licentia poetica* in the Management of this Dramatic Piece; and deviates, in a particular or two, from what is agreed on by Historians: The Queen *Thermusa* being not the Wife of King *Artabanus*, but (according to *Tacitus*, *Strabo* and *Josephus*) of *Phraates*; *Artabanus* being the fourth King of *Parthia* after him. Such Lapses are not unprecedented among the Poets; and will the more readily admit of an Excuse, when the Voice of History is followed in the Description of Characters.

DRAMATIS PERSONÆ

MEN.

ARTABANUS, King of Parthia.

ARSACES,

VARDANES } his Sons.

GOTARZES,

BARZAPHERNES, Lieutenant-Generales, under Arsac.

LYSIAS,

} Officers at Court.

PHRAATES,

BETHAS, a Noble Captive.

WOMEN.

THERMUSA, the Queen.

EVANTHE, belov'd by Arsaces.

CLEONE, her Confident.

EDESSA, Attendant on the Queen.

Guards and Attendants.

SCENE, *Ctesiphon.*

THE PRINCE OF PARTHIA
A TRAGEDY

ACT I.

SCENE I. *The Temple of the Sun.*

GOTARZES *and* PHRAATES.

GOTARZES.

He comes, Arsaces comes, my gallant Brother(Like shining Mars in all the pomp of conquest)Triumphant enters now our joyful gates;Bright Victory waits on his glitt'ring car,And shews her fav'rite to the wond'ring croud;While Fame exulting sounds the happy nameTo realms remote, and bids the world admire.Oh! 'tis a glorious day:—let none presumeT'indulge the tear, or wear the gloom of sorrow;This day shall shine in Ages yet to come,And grace the Parthian story.

PHRAATES.

Glad Ctes'phonPours forth her numbers, like a rolling deluge,To meet the blooming Hero; all the ways,On either side, as far as sight can stretch,Are lin'd with crouds, and on the lofty wallsInnumerable multitudes are rang'd.On ev'ry countenance impatience sateWith roving eye, before the train appear'd.But when they saw the Darling of the Fates,They rent the air with loud repeated shouts;The Mother shew'd him to her infant Son,And taught his lisping tongue to name Arsaces:E'en aged Sires, whose sounds are scarcely heard,By feeble strength supported, tost their caps,And gave their murmur to the gen'ral voice.

GOTARZES.

The spacious streets, which lead up to the Temple,Are strew'd with flow'rs; each, with frantic joy,His garland forms, and throws it in the way.What pleasure, Phraates, must swell his bosom,To see the prostrate nation all around him,And know he's made them happy! to hear themTease the Gods, to show'r their blessings on him!Happy Arsaces! fain I'd imitateThy matchless worth, and be a shining joy!

PHRAATES.

Hark! what a shout was that which pierc'd the skies!It seem'd as tho' all Nature's beings join'd,To hail thy glorious Brother.

GOTARZES.

Happy Parthia!Now proud Arabia dreads her destin'd chains,While shame and rout disperses all her sons.Barzaphernes pursues the fugitives,The few whom fav'ring Night redeem'd from slaughter;Swiftly they fled, for fear had wing'd their speed,And made them bless the shade which saf'ty gave.

PHRAATES.

What a bright hope is ours, when those dread pow'rsWho rule yon heav'n, and guide the mov'ments here,Shall call your royal Father to their joys:In blest Arsaces ev'ry virtue meets;He's gen'rous, brave, and wise, and good,Has skill to act, and noble fortitudeTo face bold danger, in the battle firm,And dauntless as a Lion fronts his foe.Yet is he sway'd by ev'ry tender passion,Forgiving mercy, gentleness and love;Which speak the Hero friend of humankind.

GOTARZES.

And let me speak, for 'tis to him I oweThat here I stand, and breath the common air,And 'tis my pride to tell it to the world.One luckless day as in the eager chaceMy Courser wildly bore me from the rest,A monst'rous Leopard from a bosky fenRush'd forth, and foaming lash'd the ground,And fiercely ey'd me as his destin'd quarry.My jav'lin swift I threw, but o'er his headIt erring pass'd, and harmless in the airSpent all its force; my falchin then I seiz'd,Advancing to attack my ireful foe,When furiously the savage sprung upon me,And tore me to the ground; my treach'rous bladeAbove my hand snap'd short, and left me quiteDefenceless to his rage; Arsaces then,Hearing the din, flew like some pitying pow'r,And quickly freed me from the Monster's paws,Drenching his bright lance in his spotted breast.

PHRAATES.

How diff'rent he from arrogant Vardanes?That haughty Prince eyes with a stern contemptAll other Mortals, and with lofty mienHe treads the earth as tho' he were a God.Nay, I believe that his ambitious soul,Had it but pow'r to its licentious wishes,Would dare dispute with Jove the rule of heav'n;Like a Titanian son with giant insolence,Match with the Gods, and wage immortal war,'Til their red wrath should hurl him headlong down,E'en to destruction's lowest pit of horror.

GOTARZES.

Methinks he wears not that becoming joyWhich on this bright occasion gilds the court;His brow's contracted with a gloomy frown,Pensive he stalks along, and seems a preyTo pining discontent.

PHRAATES.

Arsaces he dislikes,For standing 'twixt him, and the hope of Empire;While Envy, like a rav'nous Vulture, tearsHis canker'd heart, to see your Brother's triumph.

GOTARZES.

And yet Vardanes owes that hated BrotherAs much as I; 'twas summer last, as weWere bathing in Euphrates' flood, VardanesProud of strength would seek the further shore;But ere he the mid-stream gain'd, a poignant painShot thro' his well-strung nerves, contracting all,And the stiff joints refus'd their wonted aid.Loudly he cry'd for help, Arsaces heard,And thro' the swelling waves he rush'd to saveHis drowning Brother, and gave him life,And for the boon the Ingrate pays him hate.

PHRAATES.

There's something in the wind, for I've observ'dOf late he much frequents the Queen's apartment,And fain would court her favour, wild is sheTo gain revenge for fell Vonones' death,And firm resolves the ruin of Arsaces.Because that fill'd with filial piety,To save his Royal Sire, he struck the boldPresumptuous Traitor dead; nor heeds sheThe hand which gave her Liberty, nay rais'd herAgain to Royalty.

GOTARZES.

Ingratitude,Thou hell-born fiend, how horrid is thy form!The Gods sure let thee loose to scourge mankind,And save them from an endless waste of thunder.

PHRAATES.

Yet I've beheld this now so haughty Queen,Bent with distress, and e'en by pride forsook,When following thy Sire's triumphant car,Her tears and ravings mov'd the senseless herd,And pity blest their more than savage breasts,With the short pleasure of a moment's softness.Thy Father, conquer'd by her charms (for whatCan charm like mourning beauty), soon struck offHer chains, and rais'd her to his bed and throne.Adorn'd the brows of her aspiring Son,The fierce Vonones, with the regal crownOf rich Armenia, once the happy ruleOf Tisaphernes, her deceased Lord.

GOTARZES.

And he in wasteful war return'd his thanks,Refus'd the homage he had sworn to pay,And spread Destruction ev'ry where around,'Til from Arsaces' hand he met the fateHis crimes deserv'd.

PHRAATES.

As yet your princely BrotherHas scap'd Thermusa's rage, for still residingIn peaceful times, within his Province, ne'erHas fortune blest her with a sight of him,On whom she'd wreck her vengeance.

GOTARZES.

She has wonBy spells, I think, so much on my fond father,That he is guided by her will alone.She rules the realm, her pleasure is a law,All offices and favours are bestow'd,As she directs.

PHRAATES.

But see, the Prince, Vardanes,Proud Lysias with him, he whose soul is harshWith jarring discord. Nought but madding rage,And ruffian-like revenge his breast can know,Indeed to gain a point he'll condescendTo mask the native rancour of his heart,And smooth his venom'd tongue with flattery.Assiduous now he courts Vardanes' friendship,See, how he seems to answer all his gloom,And give him frown for frown.

GOTARZES.

Let us retire,And shun them now; I know not what it means,But chilling horror shivers o'er my limbs,When Lysias I behold.—

SCENE II. VARDANES *and* LYSIAS.

LYSIAS.

That shout proclaims

[*Shout.*

Arsaces' near approach.

VARDANES.

Peace, prithee, peace,Wilt thou still shock me with that hated sound,And grate harsh discord in my offended ear?If thou art fond of echoing the name,Join with the servile croud, and hail his triumph.

LYSIAS.

I hail him? By our glorious shining God,I'd sooner lose my speech, and all my daysIn silence rest, conversing with my thoughts,Than hail Arsaces.

VARDANES.

Yet, again his name,Sure there is magic in it, Parthia's drunkAnd giddy with the joy; the houses' topsWith gaping spectators are throng'd, nay wildThey climb such precipices that the eyeIs dazzl'd with their daring; ev'ry wretchWho long has been immur'd, nor dar'd enjoyThe common benefits of sun and air,Creeps from his lurking place; e'en feeble age,Long to the sickly couch confin'd, stalks forth,And with infectious breath assails the Gods.O! curse the name, the idol of their joy.

LYSIAS.

And what's that name, that thus they should disturbThe ambient air, and weary gracious heav'nWith ceaseless bellowings? Vardanes soundsWith equal harmony, and suits as wellThe loud repeated shouts of noisy joy.Can he bid Chaos Nature's rule dissolve,Can he deprive mankind of light and day,And turn the Seasons from their destin'd course?Say, can he do all this, and be a God?If not, what is his matchless merit? What dares he,Vardanes dares not? blush not, noble Prince,For praise is merit's due, and I will give it;E'en 'mid the croud which waits thy Brother's smile,I'd loud proclaim the merit of Vardanes.

VARDANES.

Forbear this warmth, your friendship urges far.Yet know your love shall e'er retain a placeIn my remembrance. There is something here—

[*Pointing to his breast.*

Another time and I will give thee all;But now, no more.—

LYSIAS.

You may command my services,I'm happy to obey. Of late your BrotherDelights in hind'ring my advancement,And ev'ry boaster's rais'd above my merit,Barzaphernes alone commands his ear,His oracle in all.

VARDANES.

I hate Arsaces,Tho' he's my Mother's son, and churchmen sayThere's something sacred in the name of Brother.My soul endures him not, and he's the baneOf all my hopes of greatness. Like the sunHe rules the day, and like the night's pale Queen,My fainter beams are lost when he appears.And this because he came into the world,A moon or two before me: What's the diff'rence,That he alone should shine in Empire's seat?I am not apt to trumpet forth my praise,Or highly name myself, but this I'll speak,To him in ought, I'm not the least inferior.Ambition, glorious fever! mark of Kings,Gave me immortal thirst and rule of Empire.Why lag'd my tardy soul, why droop'd the wing,Nor forward springing, shot before his speedTo seize the prize?—'Twas Empire—Oh! 'twas Empire—

LYSIAS.

Yet, I must think that of superior mouldYour soul was form'd, fit for a heav'nly state,And left reluctant its sublime abode,And painfully obey'd the dread command,When Jove's controuling fate forc'd it below.His soul was earthly, and it downward mov'd,Swift as to the center of attraction.

VARDANES.

It might be so—But I've another causeTo hate this Brother, ev'ry way my rival;In love as well as glory he's above me;I dote on fair Evanthe, but the charmerDisdains my ardent suit, like a miserHe treasures up her beauties to himself:Thus is he form'd to give me torture ever.—But hark, they've reach'd the Temple,Didst thou observe the croud, their eagerness,Each put the next aside to catch a look,Himself was elbow'd out?—Curse, curse their zeal—

LYSIAS.

Stupid folly!

VARDANES.

I'll tell thee, Lysias,This many-headed monster multitude,Unsteady is as giddy fortune's wheel,As woman fickle, varying as the wind;To-day they this way course, the next they veer,And shift another point, the next another.

LYSIAS.

Curiosity's another name for man,The blazing meteor streaming thro' the airCommands our wonder, and admiring eyes,With eager gaze we trace the lucent path,'Til spent at length it shrinks to native nothing.While the bright stars which ever steady glow,Unheeded shine, and bless the world below.

SCENE III. QUEEN *and* EDESSA.

QUEEN.

Oh! give me way, the haughty victor comes,Surrounded by adoring multitudes;On swelling tides of praise to heav'n they raise him;To deck their idol, they rob the glorious beingsOf their splendour.

EDESSA.

My royal Lady,Chace hence these passions.

QUEEN.

Peace, forever peace,Have I not cause to hate this homicide?'Twas by his cursed hand Vonones fell,Yet fell not as became his gallant spirit,Not by the warlike arm of chief renown'd,But by a youth, ye Gods, a beardless stripling,Stab'd by his dastard falchin from behind;For well I know he fear'd to meet Vonones,As princely warriors meet with open daring,But shrunk amidst his guards, and gave him death,When faint with wounds, and weary with the fight.

EDESSA.

With anguish I have heard his hapless fate,And mourn'd in silence for the gallant Prince.

QUEEN.

Soft is thy nature, but, alas! Edessa,Thy heart's a stranger to a mother's sorrows,To see the pride of all her wishes blasted;Thy fancy cannot paint the storm of grief,Despair and anguish, which my breast has known.Oh!

show'r, ye Gods, your torments on Arsaces,Curs'd be the morn which dawn'd upon his birth.

EDESSA.

Yet, I intreat—

QUEEN.

Away! for I will curse—Oh! may he never know a father's fondness,Or know it to his sorrow, may his hopesOf joy be cut like mine, and his short lifeBe one continu'd tempest; if he lives,Let him be curs'd with jealousy and fear,And vext with anguish of neglecting scorn;May tort'ring hope present the flowing cup,Then hasty snatch it from his eager thirst,And when he dies base treach'ry be the means.

EDESSA.

Oh! calm your spirits.

QUEEN.

Yes, I'll now be calm,Calm as the sea when the rude waves are laid,And nothing but a gentle swell remains;My curse is heard, and I shall have revenge;There's something here which tells me 'twill be so,And peace resumes her empire o'er my breast.Vardanes is the Minister of Vengeance;Fir'd by ambition, he aspiring seeksT'adorn his brows with Parthia's diadem;I've fann'd the fire, and wrought him up to fury,Envy shall urge him forward still to dare,And discord be the prelude to destruction,Then this detested race shall feel my hate.

EDESSA.

And doth thy hatred then extend so far,That innocent and guilty all alikeMust feel thy dreadful vengeance?

QUEEN.

Ah! Edessa,Thou dost not know e'en half my mighty wrongs,But in thy bosom I will pour my sorrows.

EDESSA.

With secrecy I ever have repaidYour confidence.

QUEEN.

I know thou hast; then hear:The changeling King who oft has kneel'd before me,And own'd no other pow'r, now treats meWith ill dissembl'd love mix'd with disdain.A newer beauty rules his faithless heart,Which only in variety is blest;Oft have I heard him, when wrapt up in sleep,And wanton fancy rais'd the mimic scene,Call with unusual fondness on Evanthe,While I have lain neglected by his side,Except sometimes in a mistaken raptureHe'd clasp me to his bosom.

EDESSA.

Oh! Madam,Let not corroding jealousy usurpYour Royal breast, unnumber'd ills attendThe wretch who entertains that fatal guest.

QUEEN.

Think not that I'll pursue its wand'ring fires,No more I'll know perplexing doubts and fears,And erring trace suspicion's endless maze,For, ah! I doubt no more.

EDESSA.

Their shouts approach.

QUEEN.

Lead me, Edessa, to some peaceful gloom,Some silent shade far from the walks of men,There shall the hop'd revenge my thoughts employ,And sooth my sorrows with the coming joy.

SCENE IV. EVANTHE *and* CLEONE.

EVANTHE.

No, I'll not meet him now, for love delightsIn the soft pleasures of the secret shade,And shuns the noise and tumult of the croud.How tedious are the hours which bring himTo my fond, panting heart! for oh! to thoseWho live in expectation of the bliss,Time slowly creeps, and ev'ry tardy minuteSeems mocking of their wishes. Say, Cleone,For you beheld the triumph, 'midst his pomp,Did he not seem to curse the empty show,The pageant greatness, enemy to love,Which held him from Evanthe? haste, to tell me,And feed my gready ear with the fond tale—Yet, hold—for I shall weary you with questions,And ne'er be satisfied—Beware, Cleone,And guard your heart from Love's delusive sweets.

CLEONE.

Is Love an ill, that thus you caution meTo shun his pow'r?

EVANTHE.

The Tyrant, my Cleone,Despotic rules, and fetters all our thoughts.Oh! wouldst thou love, then bid adieu to peace,Then fears will come, and jealousies intrude,Ravage your bosom, and disturb your quiet,E'en pleasure to excess will be a pain.Once I was free, then my exulting heartWas like a bird that hops from spray to spray,And all was innocence and mirth; but, lo!The Fowler came, and by his arts decoy'd,And soon the Wanton cag'd. Twice fifteen timesHas Cynthia dipt her horns in beams of light,Twice fifteen times has wasted all her brightness,Since first I knew to love; 'twas on that dayWhen curs'd Vonones fell upon the plain,The lovely Victor doubly conquer'd me.

CLEONE.

Forgive my boldness, Madam, if I askWhat chance first gave you to Vonones' pow'r?Curiosity thou know'st is of our sex.

EVANTHE.

That is a task will wake me to new sorrows,Yet thou attend, and I will tell thee all.Arabia gave me birth, my father heldGreat Offices at Court, and was reputedBrave, wise and loyal, by his Prince belov'd.Oft has he led his conqu'ring troops, and forc'dFrom frowning victory her awful honours.In infancy I was his only treasure,On me he wasted all his store of fondness.Oh! I could tell thee of his wond'rous goodness,His more than father's love and tenderness.But thou wouldst jeer, and say the tale was trifling;So did he dote upon me, for in childhoodMy infant charms, and artless innocenceBlest his fond age, and won on ev'ry heart.But, oh! from this sprung ev'ry future ill,This fatal beauty was the source of all.

CLEONE.

'Tis often so, for beauty is a flow'rThat tempts the hand to pluck it.

EVANTHE.

Full three timesHas scorching summer fled from cold winter'sRuthless blasts, as oft again has springIn sprightly youth drest nature in her beauties,Since bathing in Niphates'[5] silver stream,Attended only by one fav'rite maid;As we were sporting on the wanton waves,Swift from the wood a troop of horsemen rush'd,Rudely they seiz'd, and bore me trembling off,In vain Edessa with her shrieks assail'dThe heav'ns, for heav'n was deaf to both our pray'rs.The wretch whose insolent embrace confin'd me(Like thunder bursting on the guilty soul),With curs'd Vonones' voice pour'd in my earsA hateful tale of love; for he it seemsHad seen me at Arabia's royal court,And took those means to force me to his arms.

CLEONE.

Perhaps you may gain something from the CaptivesOf your lost Parents.

EVANTHE.

This I meant to try,Soon as the night hides Nature in her darkness,Veil'd in the gloom we'll steal into their prison.But, oh! perhaps e'en now my aged SireMay 'mongst the slain lie welt'ring on the field,Pierc'd like a riddle through with num'rous wounds,While parting life is quiv'ring on his lips,He may perhaps be calling on his Evanthe.Yes, ye great Pow'rs who boast the name of mercy,Ye have deny'd me to his latest moments,To all the offices of filial duty,To bind his wounds, and wash them with my tears,Is this, is this your mercy?

CLEONE.

Blame not heav'n,For heav'n is just and kind; dear Lady, driveThese black ideas from your gentle breast;Fancy delights to torture the distress'd,And fill the gloomy scene with shadowy ills,Summon your reason, and you'll soon have comfort.

EVANTHE.

Dost thou name comfort to me, my Cleone,Thou who know'st all my sorrows? plead no more,'Tis reason tells me I am doubly wretched.

CLEONE.

But hark, the music strikes, the rites begin,And, see, the doors are op'ning.

EVANTHE.

Let's retire;My heart is now too full to meet him here,Fly swift ye hours, till in his arms I'm prest,And each intruding care is hush'd to rest.

SCENE V.

The Scene draws and discovers, in the inner part of the Temple, a large image of the Sun, with an altar before it. Around Priests and Attendants.

KING, ARSACES, VARDANES, GOTARZES, PHRAATES, LYSIAS, *with* BETHAS *in chains.*

HYMN.

Parent of Light, to thee belongOur grateful tributary songs;Each thankful voice to thee shall rise,And chearful pierce the azure skies;While in thy praise all earth combines,And Echo in the Chorus joins.

All the gay pride of blooming May,The Lily fair and blushing Rose,To thee their early honours pay,And all their heav'nly sweets disclose.The feather'd Choir on ev'ry treeTo hail thy glorious dawn repair,While the sweet sons of harmonyWith Hallelujahs fill the air.

'Tis thou hast brac'd the Hero's arm,And giv'n the Love of praise to warmHis bosom, as he onward flies,And for his Country bravely dies.Thine's victory, and from thee springsAmbition's fire, which glows in Kings.

KING [*coming forward*].

Thus, to the Gods our tributary songs,And now, oh! let me welcome once againMy blooming victor to his Father's arms;And let me thank thee for our safety: ParthiaShall thank thee too, and give her grateful praiseTo her Deliverer.

OMNES.

All hail! Arsaces!

KING.

Thanks to my loyal friends.

VARDANES [*aside*].

Curse, curse the sound,E'en Echo gives it back with int'rest,The joyful gales swell with the pleasing theme,And waft it far away to distant hills.O that my breath was poison, then indeedI'd hail him like the rest, but blast him too.

ARSACES.

My Royal Sire, these honours are unmerited,Beneath your prosp'rous auspices I fought,Bright vict'ry to your banners joyful flew,And favour'd for the Sire the happy son.But lenity should grace the victor's laurels,Then, here, my gracious Father—

KING.

Ha! 'tis Bethas!Know'st thou, vain wretch, what fate attends on thoseWho dare oppose the pow'r of mighty Kings,Whom heav'n delights to favour? sure some GodWho sought to punish you for impious deeds,'Twas urg'd you forward to insult our arms,And brave us at our Royal City's gates.

BETHAS.

At honour's call, and at my King's command,Tho' it were even with my single arm, againI'd brave the multitude, which, like a deluge,O'erwhelm'd my gallant handful; yea, wou'd meetUndaunted, all the fury of the torrent.'Tis honour is the guide of all my actions,The ruling star by which I steer thro' life,And shun the shelves of infamy and vice.

KING.

It was the thirst of gain which drew you on;'Tis thus that Av'rice always cloaks its views,Th' ambition of your Prince you gladly snatch'dAs opportunity to fill your coffers.It was the plunder of our palaces,And of our wealthy cities, fill'd your dreams,And urg'd you on your way; but you have metThe due reward of your audacity.Now shake your chains, shake and delight your earsWith the soft music of your golden fetters.

BETHAS.

True, I am fall'n, but glorious was my fall,The day was brav'ly fought, we did our best,But victory's of heav'n. Look o'er yon field,See if thou findest one Arabian backDisfigur'd with dishonourable wounds.No, here, deep on their bosoms, are engrav'dThe marks of honour! 'twas thro' here their soulsFlew to their blissful seats. Oh! why did ISurvive the fatal day? To be this slave,To be the gaze and sport of vulgar crouds,Thus, like a shackl'd tyger, stalk my round,And grimly low'r upon the shouting herd.Ye Gods!—

KING.

Away with him to instant death.

ARSACES.

Hear me, my Lord, O, not on this bright day,Let not this day of joy blush with his blood.Nor count his steady loyalty a crime,But give him life, Arsaces humbly asks it,And may you e'er be serv'd with honest hearts.

KING.

Well, be it so; hence, bear him to his dungeon;Lysias, we here commit him to thy charge.

BETHAS.

Welcome my dungeon, but more welcome death.Trust not too much, vain Monarch, to your pow'r,Know fortune places all her choicest giftsOn ticklish heights, they shake with ev'ry breeze,And oft some rude wind hurls them to the ground.Jove's thunder strikes the lofty palaces,While the low cottage, in humility,Securely stands, and sees the mighty ruin.What King can boast, to-morrow as to-day,Thus, happy will I reign? The rising sunMay view him seated on a splendid throne,And, setting, see him shake the servile chain.

[*Exit guarded.*

SCENE VI.

KING, ARSACES, VARDANES, GOTARZES, PHRAATES.

GOTARZES.

Thus let me hail thee from the croud distinct,For in the exulting voice of gen'ral joyMy fainter sounds were lost, believe me, Brother,My soul dilates with joy to see thee thus.

ARSACES.

Thus let me thank thee in this fond embrace.

VARDANES.

The next will be my turn, Gods, I had ratherBe circl'd in a venom'd serpent's fold.

GOTARZES.

O, my lov'd Brother, 'tis my humble boon,That, when the war next calls you to the field,I may attend you in the rage of battle.By imitating thy heroic deeds,Perhaps, I may rise to some little worth,Beneath thy care I'll try my feeble wings,Till taught by thee to soar to nobler heights.

KING.

Why, that's my boy, thy spirit speaks thy birth,No more I'll turn thee from the road to glory,To rust in slothfulness, with lazy Gownsmen.

GOTARZES.

Thanks, to my Sire, I'm now completely blest.

ARSACES.

But, I've another Brother, where's Vardanes?

KING.

Ha! what, methinks, he lurks behind the croud,And wears a gloom which suits not with the time.

VARDANES.

Doubt not my Love, tho' I lack eloquence,To dress my sentiments and catch the ear,Tho' plain my manners, and my language rude,My honest heart disdains to wear disguise.Then think not I am slothful in the race,Or, that my Brother springs before my Love.

ARSACES.

Far be suspicion from me.

VARDANES.

So, 'tis done,Thanks to dissembling, all is well again.

KING.

Now let us forward, to the Temple go,And let, with chearful wine, the goblets flow;Let blink-ey'd Jollity his aid afford,To crown our triumph, round the festive board:But, let the wretch, whose soul can know a care,Far from our joys, to some lone shade repair,In secrecy, there let him e'er remain,Brood o'er his gloom, and still increase his pain.

End of the First Act.

ACT II.

SCENE I. *A Prison.*

LYSIAS [*alone*].

The Sun set frowning, and refreshing EveLost all its sweets, obscur'd in double gloom.This night shall sleep be stranger to these eyes,Peace dwells not here, and slumber flies the shock;My spirits, like the elements, are warring,And mock the tempest with a kindred rage—I, who can joy in nothing, but revenge,Know not those boasted ties of Love and Friendship;Vardanes I regard, but as he give meSome hopes of vengeance on the Prince Arsaces—But, ha! he comes, wak'd by the angry storm,'Tis to my wish, thus would I form designs,Horror should breed beneath the veil of horror,And darkness aid conspiracies—He's here—

SCENE II. VARDANES *and* LYSIAS.

LYSIAS.

Welcome, my noble Prince.

VARDANES.

Thanks, gentle friend;Heav'ns! what a night is this!

LYSIAS.

'Tis fill'd with terror;Some dread event beneath this horror lurks,Ordain'd by fate's irrevocable doom;Perhaps Arsaces' fall—and angry heav'nSpeaks it, in thunder, to the trembling world.

VARDANES.

Terror indeed! it seems as sick'ning NatureHad giv'n her order up to gen'ral ruin;The Heav'ns appear as one continu'd flame,Earth with her terror shakes, dim night retires,And the red lightning gives a dreadful day,While in the thunder's voice each sound is lost;Fear sinks the panting heart in ev'ry bosom,E'en the pale dead, affrighted at the horror,As tho' unsafe, start from their marble goals,And howling thro' the streets are seeking shelter.

LYSIAS.

I saw a flash stream thro' the angry clouds,And bend its course to where a stately pineBehind the garden stood, quickly it seiz'd,And wrapt it in a fiery fold, the trunkWas shiver'd into atoms, and the branchesOff were lopt, and wildly scatter'd round.

VARDANES.

Why rage the elements, they are not curs'dLike me? Evanthe frowns not angry on them,The wind may play upon her beauteous bosomNor fear her chiding, light can bless her sense,And in the floating mirror she beholdsThose beauties which can fetter all mankind.Earth gives her joy, she plucks the fragrant rose,Pleas'd takes its sweets, and gazes on its bloom.

LYSIAS.

My Lord, forget her, tear her from your breast.Who, like the Phœnix gazes on the sun,And strives to soar up to the glorious blaze,Should never leave Ambition's brightest object,To turn, and view the beauties of a flow'r.

VARDANES.

O, Lysias, chide no more, for I have done.Yes, I'll forget this proud disdainful beauty;Hence, with vain love—Ambition, now, alone,Shall guide my actions, since mankind delightsTo give me pain, I'll study mischief too,And shake the earth, e'en like this raging tempest.

LYSIAS.

A night like this, so dreadful to behold,Since my remembrance's birth, I never saw.

VARDANES.

E'en such a night, dreadful as this, they say,My teeming Mother gave me to the world.Whence by those sages who, in knowledge rich,Can pry into futurity, and tellWhat distant ages will produce of wonder,My days were deem'd to be a hurricane;My early life prov'd their prediction false;Beneath a sky serene my voyage began,But, to this long uninterrupted calm,Storms shall succeed.

LYSIAS.

Then haste, to raise the tempest;My soul disdains this one eternal round,Where each succeeding day is like the former.Trust me, my noble Prince, here is a heartSteady and firm to all your purposes,And here's a hand that knows to executeWhate'er designs thy daring breast can form,Nor ever shake with fear.

VARDANES.

And I will use it,Come to my bosom, let me place thee here,How happy am I clasping so much virtue!Now, by the light, it is my firm belief,One mighty soul in common swells our bosoms,Such sameness can't be match'd in diff'rent beings.

LYSIAS.

Your confidence, my Lord, much honours me,And when I act unworthy of your loveMay I be hooted from Society,As tho' disgraceful to the human kind,And driv'n to herd among the savage race.

VARDANES.

Believe me, Lysias, I do not knowA single thought which tends toward suspicion,For well I know thy worth, when I affront it,By the least doubt, may I be ever curs'dWith faithless friends, and by his dagger fallWhom my deluded wishes most would favour.

LYSIAS.

Then let's no longer trifle time away,I'm all impatience till I see thy browsBright in the glories of a diadem;My soul is fill'd with anguish when I thinkThat by weak Princes worn, 'tis thus disgrac'd.Haste, mount the throne, and, like the morning Sun,Chace with your piercing beams those mists away,Which dim the glory of the Parthian state:Each honest heart desires it, numbers there areReady to join you, and support your cause,Against th' opposing faction.

VARDANES.

Sure some God,Bid you thus call me to my dawning honours,And joyful I obey the pleasing summons.Now by the pow'rs of heav'n, of earth and hell,Most solemnly I swear, I will not knowThat quietude which I was wont to know,'Til I have climb'd the height of all my wishes,Or fell, from glory, to the silent grave.

LYSIAS.

Nobly resolv'd, and spoken like Vardanes,There shone my Prince in his superior lustre.

VARDANES.

But, then, Arsaces, he's a fatal bar—O! could I brush this busy insect from me,Which envious strives to rob me of my bloom,Then might I, like some fragrant op'ning flow'r,Spread all my beauties in the face of day.Ye Gods! why did ye give me such a soul(A soul, which ev'ry way is form'd for Empire),And damn me with a younger Brother's right?The diadem would set as well on mine,As on the brows of any lordly He;Nor is this hand weak to enforce command.And shall I steal into my grave, and giveMy name up to oblivion, to be thrownAmong the common rubbish of the times?No: Perish first, this happy hated Brother.

LYSIAS.

I always wear a dagger, for your service,I need not speak the rest—When humbly I intreated of your BrotherT' attend him as Lieutenant in this war,Frowning contempt, he haughtily reply'd,He entertain'd not Traitors in his service.True, I betray'd Orodes, but with cause,He struck me, like a sorry abject slave,And still withheld from giving what he'd promis'd.Fear not Arsaces, believe me, he shallSoon his Quietus have—But, see, he comes,—What can this mean? Why at this lonely hour,And unattended?—Ha! 'tis opportune—I'll in, and stab him now. I heed not whatThe danger is, so I but have revenge,Then heap perdition on me.

VARDANES.

Hold, awhile—'Twould be better could we undermine him,And make him fall by Artabanus' doom.

LYSIAS.

Well, be it so—

VARDANES.

But let us now retire,We must not be observ'd together here.

SCENE III.

ARSACES [*alone*].

'Tis here that hapless Bethas is confin'd;He who, but yesterday, like angry Jove,When punishing the crimes of guilty men,Spread death and desolation all around,While Parthia trembl'd at his name; is nowUnfriended and forlorn, and counts the hours,Wrapt in the gloomy horrors of a goal.—How dark, and hidden, are the turns of fate!His rigid fortune moves me to compassion.O! 'tis a heav'nly virtue when the heartCan feel the sorrows of another's bosom,It dignifies the man: The stupid wretchWho knows not this sensation, is an image,And wants the feeling to make up a life—I'll in, and give my aid to sooth his sorrows.

SCENE IV.

VARDANES *and* LYSIAS.

LYSIAS.

Let us observe with care, something we, yet,May gather, to give to us the vantage;No matter what's the intent.

VARDANES.

How easy 'tisTo cheat this busy, tattling, censuring world!For fame still names our actions, good or bad,As introduc'd by chance, which ofttimes throwsWrong lights on objects; vice she dresses up—In the bright form, and goodliness, of virtue,While virtue languishes, and pines neglected,Rob'd of her lustre—But, let's forward, Lysias—Thou know'st each turn in this thy dreary rule,Then lead me to some secret stand, from whence,Unnotic'd, all their actions we may view.

LYSIAS.

Here, take your stand behind—See, Bethas comes.

[*They retire.*

SCENE V.

BETHAS [*alone*].

To think on Death in gloomy solitude,In dungeons and in chains, when expectationJoin'd with serious thought describe him to us,His height'n'd terrors strike upon the soulWith awful dread; imagination rais'dTo frenzy, plunges in a sea of horror,And tastes the pains, the agonies of dying—Ha! who is this, perhaps he bears my fate?It must be so, but, why this privacy?

SCENE VI.

ARSACES *and* BETHAS.

ARSACES.

Health to the noble Bethas, health and joy!

BETHAS.

A steady harden'd villain, one experienc'dIn his employment; ha! where's thy dagger?It cannot give me fear; I'm ready, see,My op'ning bosom tempts the friendly steel.Fain would I cast this tiresome being off,Like an old garment worn to wretchedness.Here, strike for I'm prepar'd.

ARSACES.

Oh! view me better,Say, do I wear the gloomy ruffian's frown?

BETHAS.

Ha! 'tis the gallant Prince, the brave Arsaces,And Bethas' Conqueror.

ARSACES.

And Bethas' friend,A name I'm proud to wear.

BETHAS.

Away—away—Mock with your jester to divert the court,Fit Scene for sportive joys and frolic mirth;Think'st thou I lack that manly constancyWhich braves misfortune, and remains unshaken?Are these, are these the emblems of thy friendship,These rankling chains, say, does it gall like these?No, let me taste the bitterness of sorrow,For I am reconcil'd to wretchedness.The Gods have empty'd all their mighty store,Of hoarded Ills, upon my whiten'd age;Now death—but, oh! I court coy death in vain,Like a cold maid, he scorns my fond complaining.'Tis thou, insulting Prince, 'tis thou hast dragg'dMy soul, just rising, down again to earth,And clogg'd her wings with dull mortality,A hateful bondage! Why—

ARSACES.

A moment hear me—

BETHAS.

Why dost thou, like an angry vengeful ghost,Glide hither to disturb this peaceful gloom?What, dost thou envy me my miseries,My chains and flinty pavement, where I oftIn sleep behold the image of the death I wish,Forget my sorrows and heart-breaking anguish?These horrors I would undisturb'd enjoy,Attended only by my silent thoughts;Is it to see the wretch that you have made;To view the ruins of unhappy Bethas,And triumph in my grief? Is it for thisYou penetrate my dark joyless prison?

ARSACES.

Oh! do not injure me by such suspicions.Unknown to me are cruel scoffs and jests;My breast can feel compassion's tenderness,The warrior's warmth, the soothing joys of friendship.When adverse bold battalions shook the earth,And horror triumph'd on the hostile field,I sought you with a glorious enmity,And arm'd my brow with the stern frown of war.But now the angry trumpet wakes no moreThe youthful champion to the lust for blood.Retiring rage gives place to softer passions,And gen'rous warriors know no longer hate,The name of foe is lost, and thus I askYour friendship.

BETHAS.

Ah! why dost thou mock me thus?

ARSACES.

Let the base coward, he who ever shrinks,And trembles, at the slight name of danger,Taunt, and revile, with bitter gibes, the wretched;The brave are ever to distress a friend.Tho' my dear country (spoil'd by wasteful war,Her harvests blazing, desolate her towns,And baleful ruin shew'd her haggard face)Call'd out on me to save her from her foes,And I obey'd, yet to your gallant prowess,And unmatch'd deeds, I admiration gave.But now my country knows the sweets of safety,Freed from her fears; sure now I may indulgeMy just esteem for your superior virtue.

BETHAS.

Yes, I must think you what you would be thought,For honest minds are easy of belief,And always judge of others by themselves,But often are deceiv'd; yet Parthia breeds notVirtue much like thine, the barb'rous clime teemsWith nought else but villains vers'd in ill.

ARSACES.

Dissimulation never mark'd my looks,Nor flatt'ring deceit e'er taught my tongue,The tale of falsehood, to disguise my thoughts:To Virtue, and her fair companion, Truth,I've ever bow'd, their holy precepts kept,And scann'd by them the actions of my life.Suspicion surely ne'er disturbs the brave,They never know the fears of doubting thoughts;But free, as are the altars of the Gods,From ev'ry hand receive the sacrifice.

SCENE VII.

ARSACES, BETHAS, EVANTHE *and* CLEONE.

EVANTHE.

Heav'ns! what a gloom hangs round this dreadful place,Fit habitation for the guilty mind!Oh! if such terrors wait the innocent,Which tread these vaults, what must the impious feel,Who've all their crimes to stare them in the face?

BETHAS.

Immortal Gods! is this reality?Or mere illusion? am I blest at last,Or is it to torment me that you've rais'dThis semblance of Evanthe to my eyes?It is! it is! 'tis she!—

ARSACES.

Ha!—what means this?—She faints! she faints! life has forsook its seat,Pale Death usurps its place—Evanthe, Oh!Awake to life!—Love and Arsaces call!—

BETHAS.

Off—give her to my arms, my warm embraceShall melt Death's icy chains.

CLEONE.

She lives! she lives!—See, on her cheeks the rosy glow returns.

ARSACES.

O joy! O joy! her op'ning eyes, again,Break, like the morning sun, a better day.

BETHAS.

Evanthe!—

EVANTHE.

Oh! my Father!—

ARSACES.

Ha!—her Father!

BETHAS.

Heav'n thou art kind at last, and this indeedIs recompense for all the ills I've past;For all the sorrows which my heart has known,Each wakeful night, and ev'ry day of anguish.This, this has sweet'n'd all my bitter cup,And gave me once again to taste of joy,Joy which has long been stranger to this bosom.Hence—hence disgrace—off, ignominy off—But one embrace—I ask but one embrace,And 'tis deny'd.

EVANTHE.

Oh, yes, around thy neckI'll fold my longing arms, thy softer fetters,Thus press thee to my happy breast, and kissAway those tears that stain thy aged cheeks.

BETHAS.

Oh! 'tis too much! it is too much! ye Gods!Life's at her utmost stretch, and bursting nearWith heart-swoln ecstasy; now let me die.

ARSACES.

What marble heartCould see this scene unmov'd, nor give a tear?My eyes grow dim, and sympathetic passionFalls like a gushing torrent on my bosom.

EVANTHE.

O! happy me, this place, which lately seem'dSo fill'd with horror, now is pleasure's circle.Here will I fix my seat; my pleasing taskShall be to cherish thy remaining life.All night I'll keep a vigil o'er thy slumbers,And on my breast repose thee, mark thy dreams,And when thou wak'st invent some pleasing tale,Or with my songs the tedious hours beguile.

BETHAS.

Still let me gaze, still let me gaze upon thee,Let me strain ev'ry nerve with ravishment,And all my life be center'd in my vision.To see thee thus, to hear thy angel voice,It is, indeed, a luxury of pleasure!—Speak, speak again, for oh! 'tis heav'n to hear thee!Celestial sweetness dwells on ev'ry accent;—Lull me to rest, and sooth my raging joy.Joy which distracts me with unruly transports.Now, by thy dear departed Mother's shade,Thou brightest pattern of all excellence,Thou who in prattling infancy hast blest me,I wou'd not give this one transporting moment,This fullness of delight, for all—but, ah!'Tis vile, Ambition, Glory, all is vile,To the soft sweets of love and tenderness.

EVANTHE.

Now let me speak, my throbbing heart is full,I'll tell thee all—alas! I have forgot—'T 'as slipt me in the tumult of my joy.And yet I thought that I had much to say.

BETHAS.

Oh! I have curs'd my birth, indeed, I haveBlasphem'd the Gods, with unbecoming passion,Arraign'd their Justice, and defy'd their pow'r,In bitterness, because they had deny'dThee to support the weakness of my age.But now no more I'll rail and rave at fate,All its decrees are just, complaints are impious,Whate'er short-sighted mortals feel, springs fromTheir blindness in the ways of Providence;Sufficient wisdom 'tis for man to knowThat the great Ruler is e'er wise and good.

ARSACES.

Ye figur'd stones!Ye senseless, lifeless images of men,Who never gave a tear to others' woe,Whose bosoms never glow'd for others' good,O weary heav'n with your repeated pray'rs,And strive to melt the angry pow'rs to pity,That ye may truly live.

EVANTHE.

Oh! how my heartBeats in my breast, and shakes my trembling frame!I sink beneath this sudden flood of joy,Too mighty for my spirits.

ARSACES.

My Evanthe,Thus in my arms I catch thy falling beauties,Chear thee; and kiss thee back to life again:Thus to my bosom I could ever hold thee,And find new pleasure.

EVANTHE.

O! my lov'd Arsaces,Forgive me that I saw thee not before,Indeed my soul was busily employ'd,Nor left a single thought at liberty.But thou, I know, art gentleness and love.Now I am doubly paid for all my sorrows,For all my fears for thee.

ARSACES.

Then, fear no more:Give to guilty wretches painful terrors:Whose keen remembrance raises horrid forms,Shapes that in spite of nature shock their soulsWith dreadful anguish: but thy gentle bosom,Where innocence beams light and gayety,Can never know a fear, now shining joyShall gild the pleasing scene.

EVANTHE.

Alas! this joyI fear is like a sudden flame shot fromTh' expiring taper, darkness will ensue,And double night I dread enclose us round.Anxiety does yet disturb my breast,And frightful apprehension shakes my soul.

BETHAS.

How shall I thank you, ye bright glorious beings!Shall I in humble adoration bow,Or fill the earth with your resounding praise?No, this I leave to noisy hypocrites,A Mortal's tongue disgraces such a theme;But heav'n delights where silent gratitudeMounts each aspiring thought to its bright throne,Nor leaves to language aught; words may indeedFrom man to man their sev'ral wants express,Heav'n asks the purer incense of the heart.

ARSACES.

I'll to the King, ere he retires to rest,Nor will I leave him 'til I've gain'd your freedom;His love will surely not deny me this.

SCENE VIII.

VARDANES *and* LYSIAS *come forward.*

LYSIAS.

'Twas a moving scene, e'en my rough natureWas nighly melted.

VARDANES.

Hence coward pity—What is joy to them, to me is torture.Now am I rack'd with pains that far exceedThose agonies, which fabling Priests relate,The damn'd endure: The shock of hopeless Love,Unblest with any views to sooth ambition,Rob me of all my reas'ning faculties.Arsaces gains Evanthe, fills the throne,While I am doom'd to foul obscurity,To pine and grieve neglected.

LYSIAS.

My noble Prince,Would it not be a master-piece, indeed,To make this very bliss their greatest ill,And damn them in the very folds of joy?

VARDANES.

This I will try, and stretch my utmost art,Unknown is yet the means—We'll think on that—Success may follow if you'll lend your aid.

LYSIAS.

The storm still rages—I must to the King,And know what further orders ere he sleeps:Soon I'll return, and speak my mind more fully.

VARDANES.

Haste, Lysias, haste, to aid me with thy council;For without thee, all my designs will proveLike night and chaos, darkness and confusion;But to thy word shall light and order spring.—Let coward Schoolmen talk of Virtue's rules,And preach the vain Philosophy of fools;Court eager their obscurity, afraidTo taste a joy, and in some gloomy shadeDream o'er their lives, while in a mournful strainThey sing of happiness they never gain.But form'd for nobler purposes I come,To gain a crown, or else a glorious tomb.

End of the Second Act.

ACT III.

SCENE I. *The Palace.*

QUEEN *and* EDESSA.

QUEEN.

Talk not of sleep to me, the God of RestDisdains to visit where disorder reigns;Not beds of down, nor music's softest strains,Can charm him when 'tis anarchy within.He flies with eager haste the mind disturb'd,And sheds his blessings where the soul's in peace.

EDESSA.

Yet, hear me, Madam!

QUEEN.

Hence, away, Edessa,For thou know'st not the pangs of jealousy.Say, has he not forsook my bed, and left meLike a lone widow mourning to the night?This, with the injury his son has done me,If I forgive, may heav'n in anger show'rIts torments on me—Ha! isn't that the King!

EDESSA.

It is your Royal Lord, great Artabanus.

QUEEN.

Leave me, for I would meet him here alone,Something is lab'ring in my breast—

SCENE II.

KING *and* QUEEN.

KING.

This leadsTo fair Evanthe's chamber—Ha! the Queen.

QUEEN.

Why dost thou start? so starts the guilty wretch,When, by some watchful eye, prevented fromHis dark designs.

KING.

Prevented! how, what mean'st thou?

QUEEN.

Art thou then so dull? cannot thy heart,Thy changeling heart, explain my meaning to thee,Or must upbraiding 'wake thy apprehension?Ah! faithless, tell me, have I lost those charmsWhich thou so oft hast sworn could warm old age,And tempt the frozen hermit from his cell,To visit once again our gayer world?This, thou hast sworn, perfidious as thou art,A thousand times; as often hast thou swornEternal constancy, and endless love,Yet ev'ry time was perjur'd.

KING.

Sure, 'tis frenzy.

QUEEN.

Indeed, 'tis frenzy, 'tis the height of madness,For I have wander'd long in sweet delusion.At length the pleasing Phantom chang'd its form,And left me in a wilderness of woe.

KING.

Prithee, no more, dismiss those jealous heats;Love must decay, and soon disgust arise,Where endless jarrings and upbraidings dampThe gentle flame, which warms the lover's breast.

QUEEN.

Oh! grant me patience heav'n! and dost thou thinkBy these reproaches to disguise thy guilt?No, 'tis in vain, thy art's too thin to hide it.

KING.

Curse on the marriage chain!—the clog, a wife,Who still will force and pall us with the joy,Tho' pow'r is wanting, and the will is cloy'd,Still urge the debt when Nothing's left to pay.

QUEEN.

Ha! dost thou own thy crime, nor feel the glowOf conscious shame?

KING.

Why should I blush, if heav'nHas made me as I am, and gave me passions?Blest only in variety, then blameThe Gods, who form'd my nature thus, not me.

QUEEN.

Oh! Traitor! Villain!

KING.

Hence—away—No more I'll wage a woman's war with words.

[*Exit.*

QUEEN.

Down, down ye rising passions, give me ease,Or break my heart, for I must yet be calm—But, yet, revenge, our Sex's joy, is mine;By all the Gods! he lives not till the morn.Who slights my love, shall sink beneath my hate.

SCENE III.

QUEEN *and* VARDANES.

VARDANES.

What, raging to the tempest?

QUEEN.

Away!—away!—Yes, I will rage—a tempest's here within,Above the trifling of the noisy elements.Blow ye loud winds, burst with your violence,For ye but barely imitate the stormThat wildly rages in my tortur'd breast—The King—the King—

VARDANES.

Ha! what?—the King?

QUEEN.

Evanthe!

VARDANES.

You talk like riddles, still obscure and short,Give me some cue to guide me thro' this maze.

QUEEN.

Ye pitying pow'rs!—oh! for a poison, someCurs'd deadly draught, that I might blast her beauties,And rob her eyes of all their fatal lustre.

VARDANES.

What, blast her charms?—dare not to think of it—Shocking impiety;—the num'rous systemsWhich gay creation spreads, bright blazing suns,With all th' attendant planets circling round,Are not worth half the radiance of her eyes.She's heav'n's peculiar care, good spir'ts hoverRound, a shining band, to guard her beauties.

QUEEN.

Be they watchful then: for should remissnessTaint the guard, I'll snatch the opportunity,And hurl her to destruction.

VARDANES.

Dread Thermusa,Say, what has rous'd this tumult in thy soul?What dost thou rage with unabating fury,Wild as the winds, loud as the troubl'd sea?

QUEEN.

Yes, I will tell thee—Evanthe—curse her—With charms—Would that my curses had the pow'rTo kill, destroy, and blast where e'er I hate,Then would I curse, still curse, till death should seizeThe dying accents on my falt'ring tongue.So should this world, and the false changeling manBe buried in one universal ruin.

VARDANES.

Still err'st thou from the purpose.

QUEEN.

Ha! 'tis so—Yes I will tell thee—for I know fond fool,Deluded wretch, thou dotest on Evanthe—Be that thy greatest curse, be curs'd like me,With jealousy and rage, for know, the King,Thy father, is thy rival.

SCENE IV.

VARDANES [*alone*].

Ha! my rival!How knew she that?—yet stay—she's gone—my rival,What then? he is Arsaces' rival too.Ha!—this may aid and ripen my designs—Could I but fire the King with jealousy,And then accuse my Brother of IntriguesAgainst the state—ha!—join'd with Bethas, andConfed'rate with th' Arabians—'tis most likelyThat jealousy would urge him to belief.I'll sink my claim until some fitter time,'Til opportunity smiles on my purpose.Lysias already has receiv'd the mandateFor Bethas' freedom: Let them still proceed,This harmony shall change to discord soon.Fortune methinks of late grows wond'rous kind,She scarcely leaves me to employ myself.

SCENE V.

KING, ARSACES, VARDANES.

KING.

But where's Evanthe? Where's the lovely Maid?

ARSACES.

On the cold pavement, by her aged Sire,The dear companion of his solitude,She sits, nor can persuasion make her rise;But in the wild extravagance of joyShe weeps, then smiles, like April's sun, thro' show'rs.While with strain'd eyes he gazes on her face,And cries, in ecstacy, "Ye gracious pow'rs!It is too much, it is too much to bear!"Then clasps her to his breast, while down his cheeksLarge drops each other trace, and mix with hers.

KING.

Thy tale is moving, for my eyes o'erflow—How slow does Lysias with Evanthe creep!So moves old time when bringing us to bliss.Now war shall cease, no more of war I'll have,Death knows satiety, and pale destructionTurns loathing from his food, thus forc'd on him.The triffling dust, the cause of all this ruin,The trade of death shall urge no more.—

SCENE VI.

KING, ARSACES, VARDANES, EVANTHE, LYSIAS.

KING.

Evanthe!—See pleasure's goddess deigns to dignifyThe happy scene, and make our bliss complete.So Venus, from her heav'nly seat, descendsTo bless the gay Cythera with her presence;A thousand smiling graces wait the goddess,A thousand little loves are flutt'ring round,And joy is mingl'd with the beauteous train.

EVANTHE.

O! Royal Sir, thus lowly to the groundI bend, in humble gratitude, acceptMy thanks, for this thy goodness, words are vileT' express the image of my lively thought,And speak the grateful fulness of my heart.All I can say, is that I now am happy,And that thy giving hand has made me blest.

KING.

O! rise, Evanthe rise, this lowly postureSuits not with charms like thine, they should command,And ev'ry heart exult in thy behests;—But, where's thy aged Sire?

EVANTHE.

This sudden turnOf fortune has so wrought upon his frame,His limbs could not support him to thy presence.

ARSACES.

This, this is truly great, this is the Hero,Like heav'n, to scatter blessings 'mong mankindAnd e'er delight in making others happy.Cold is the praise which waits the victor's triumph(Who thro' a sea of blood has rush'd to glory),To the o'erflowings of a grateful heart,By obligations conquer'd: Yet, extendThy bounty unto me.

[*Kneels.*

KING.

Ha! rise Arsaces.

ARSACES.

Not till you grant my boon.

KING.

Speak, and 'tis thine—Wide thro' our kingdom let thy eager wishesSearch for some jewel worthy of thy seeing;Something that's fit to show the donor's bounty,And by the glorious sun, our worship'd God,Thou shalt not have denial; e'en my crownShall gild thy brows with shining beams of Empire.With pleasure I'll resign to thee my honours,I long for calm retirement's softer joys.

ARSACES.

Long may you wear it, grant it bounteous heav'n,And happiness attend it; 'tis my pray'rThat daily rises with the early sweetsOf nature's incense, and the lark's loud strain.'Tis not the unruly transport of ambitionThat urges my desires to ask your crown;Let the vain wretch, who prides in gay dominion,Who thinks not of the great ones' weighty cares,Enjoy his lofty wish, wide spreading rule.The treasure which I ask, put in the scale,Would over-balance all that Kings can boast,Empire and diadems.

KING.

Away, that thought—Name it, haste—speak.

ARSACES.

For all the dang'rous toil,Thirst, hunger, marches long that I've endur'd,For all the blood I've in thy service spent,Reward me with Evanthe.

KING.

Ha! what said'st thou?—

VARDANES.

The King is mov'd, and angry bites his lip.—Thro' my benighted soul all-cheering hope

[*Aside.*

Beams, like an orient sun, reviving joy.

ARSACES.

The stern Vonones ne'er could boast a meritBut loving her.

KING.

Ah! curse the hated name—Yes, I remember when the fell ruffianDirected all his fury at my life;Then sent, by pitying heav'n, t' assert the rightOf injur'd Majesty, thou, Arsaces,Taught him the duty he ne'er knew before,And laid the Traitor dead.

ARSACES.

My Royal Sire!

LYSIAS.

My Liege, the Prince still kneels.

KING.

Ha!—rebel, off—

[*Strikes him.*

What, Lysias, did I strike thee? forgive my rage—The name of curs'd Vonones fires my blood,And gives me up to wrath.—

LYSIAS.

I am your slave,Sway'd by your pleasure—when I forget it,May this keen dagger, which I mean to hideDeep in his bosom, pierce my vitals thro'.

[*Aside.*

KING.

Didst thou not name Evanthe?

ARSACES.

I did, my Lord!And, say, whom should I name but her, in whomMy soul has center'd all her happiness?Nor canst thou blame me, view her wond'rous charms,She's all perfection; bounteous heav'n has form'd herTo be the joy, and wonder of mankind;But language is too vile to speak her beauties.Here ev'ry pow'r of glowing fancy's lost:Rose blush secure, ye lilies still enjoyYour silver whiteness, I'll not rob your charmsTo deck the bright comparison; for hereIt sure must fail.

KING.

He's wanton in her praise—

[*Aside.*

I tell thee, Prince, hadst thou as many tongues,As days have wasted since creation's birth,They were too few to tell the mighty theme.

EVANTHE.

I'm lost! I'm lost!

[*Aside.*

ARSACES.

Then I'll be dumb for ever.

KING.

O rash and fatal oath! is there no way,No winding path to shun this precipice,But must I fall and dash my hopes to atoms?In vain I strive, thought but perplexes me,Yet shews no hold to bear me up—now, holdMy heart a while—she's thine—'tis done.

ARSACES.

In deepProstration, I thank my Royal Father.

KING.

A sudden pain shoots thro' my trembling breast—Lend me thy arm Vardanes—cruel pow'rs!

SCENE VII.

ARSACES *and* EVANTHE.

EVANTHE [*after a pause*].

E'er since the dawn of my unhappy lifeJoy never shone serenely on my soul;Still something interven'd to cloud my day.Tell me, ye pow'rs, unfold the hidden crimeFor which I'm doom'd to this eternal woe,Thus still to number o'er my hours with tears?The Gods are just I know, nor are decreesIn hurry shuffl'd out, but where the boltTakes its direction justice points the mark.Yet still in vain I search within my breast,I find no sins are there to shudder at—Nought but the common frailties of our natures.Arsaces,—Oh!—

ARSACES.

Ha! why that look of anguish?Why didst thou name me with that sound of sorrow?Ah! say, why stream those gushing tears so fastFrom their bright fountain? sparkling joy should nowBe lighten'd in thine eye, and pleasure glowUpon thy rosy cheek;—ye sorrows hence—'Tis love shall triumph now.

EVANTHE.

Oh!

[*Sighs.*

ARSACES.

What means that sigh?Tell me why heaves thy breast with such emotion?Some dreadful thought is lab'ring for a vent,Haste, give it loose, ere strengthen'd by confinementIt wrecks thy frame, and tears its snowy prison.Is sorrow then so pleasing that you hoard itWith as much love, as misers do their gold?Give me my share of sorrows.

EVANTHE.

Ah! too soonYou'll know what I would hide.

ARSACES.

Be it from thee—The dreadful tale, when told by thee, shall please;Haste, to produce it with its native terrors,My steady soul shall still remain unshaken;For who when bless'd with beauties like to thineWould e'er permit a sorrow to intrude?Far hence in darksome shades does sorrow dwell,Where hapless wretches thro' the awful gloom,Echo their woes, and sighing to the winds,Augment with tears the gently murm'ring stream;But ne'er disturbs such happiness as mine.

EVANTHE.

Oh! 'tis not all thy boasted happiness,Can save thee from disquietude and care;Then build not too securely on these joys,For envious sorrow soon will undermine,And let the goodly structure fall to ruin.

ARSACES.

I charge thee, by our mutual vows, Evanthe,Tell me, nor longer keep me in suspense:Give me to know the utmost rage of fate.

EVANTHE.

Then know—impossible!—

ARSACES.

Ha! dost thou fearTo shock me?—

EVANTHE.

Know, thy Father—loves Evanthe.—

ARSACES.

Loves thee?

EVANTHE.

Yea, e'en to distraction loves me.Oft at my feet he's told the moving tale,And woo'd me with the ardency of youth.I pitied him indeed, but that was all,Thou would'st have pitied too.

ARSACES.

I fear 'tis true;A thousand crouding circumstances speak it.Ye cruel Gods! I've wreck'd a Father's peace,Oh! bitter thought!

EVANTHE.

Didst thou observe, Arsaces,How reluctant he gave me to thy arms?

ARSACES.

Yes, I observ'd that when he gave thee up,It seem'd as tho' he gave his precious life.And who'd forego the heav'n of thy love?To rest on thy soft swelling breast, and inSweet slumbers sooth each sharp intruding care?Oh! it were bliss, such as immortals taste,To press thy ruby lips distilling sweets,Or circl'd in thy snowy arms to snatchA joy, that Gods——

EVANTHE.

Come, then, my much-lov'd Prince,Let's seek the shelter of some kind retreat.Happy Arabia opens wide her arms,There may we find some friendly solitude,Far from the noise and hurry of the Court.Ambitious views shall never blast our joys,Or tyrant Fathers triumph o'er our wills:There may we live like the first happy pairCloth'd in primeval innocence secure.Our food untainted by luxurious arts,Plain, simple, as our lives, shall not destroyThe health it should sustain; while the clear brookAffords the cooling draught our thirsts to quench.There, hand in hand, we'll trace the citron grove,While with the songsters' round I join my voice,To hush thy cares and calm thy ruffl'd soul:Or, on some flow'ry bank reclin'd, my strainsShall captivate the natives of the stream,While on its crystal lap ourselves we view.

ARSACES.

I see before us a wide sea of sorrows,Th' angry waves roll forward to o'erwhelm us,Black clouds arise, and the wind whistles loud.But yet, oh! could I save thee from the wreck,Thou beauteous casket, where my joys are stor'd,Let the storm rage with double violence,Smiling I'd view its wide extended horrors.

EVANTHE.

'Tis not enough that we do know the ill,Say, shall we calmly see the tempest rise,And seek no shelter from th' inclement sky,But bid it rage?—

ARSACES.

Ha! will he force thee from me?What, tear thee from my fond and bleeding heart?And must I lose thee ever? dreadful word!Never to gaze upon thy beauties more?Never to taste the sweetness of thy lips?Never to know the joys of mutual love?Never!—Oh! let me lose the pow'r of thinking,For thought is near allied to desperation.Why, cruel Sire—why did you give me life,And load it with a weight of wretchedness?Take back my being, or relieve my sorrows—Ha! art thou not Evanthe?—Art thou notThe lovely Maid, who bless'd the fond Arsaces?—

[*Raving.*

EVANTHE.

O, my lov'd Lord, recall your scatter'd spir'ts,Alas! I fear your senses are unsettl'd.

ARSACES.

Yes, I would leave this dull and heavy sense.Let me grow mad; perhaps, I then may gainSome joy, by kind imagination form'd,Beyond reality.—O! my Evanthe!Why was I curs'd with empire? born to rule?—Would I had been some humble Peasant's son,And thou some Shepherd's daughter on the plain;My throne some hillock, and my flock my subjects,My crook my sceptre, and my faithful dogMy only guard; nor curs'd with dreams of greatness.At early dawn I'd hail the coming day,And join the lark the rival of his lay;At sultry noon to some kind shade repair,Thus joyful pass the hours, my only care,To guard my flock, and please the yielding Fair.

SCENE VIII.

KING.—VARDANES *behind the Scene.*

KING.

I will not think, to think is torment—Ha!See, how they twine! ye furies cut their hold.Now their hot blood beats loud to love's alarms;Sigh presses sigh, while from their sparkling eyesFlashes desire—Oh! ye bright heav'nly beings,Who pitying bend to suppliant Lovers' pray'rs,And aid them in extremity, assist me!

VARDANES.

Thus, for the Trojan, mourn'd the Queen of Carthage;So, on the shore she raving stood, and sawHis navy leave her hospitable shore.In vain she curs'd the wind which fill'd their sails,And bore the emblem of its change away.

[*Comes forward.*

KING.

Vardanes—Ha!—come here, I know thou lov'st me.

VARDANES.

I do, my Lord; but, say, what busy villainDurst e'er approach your ear, with coz'ning tales,And urge you to a doubt?

KING.

None, none believe me.I'll ne'er oppress thy love with fearful doubt—A little nigher—let me lean upon thee—And thou be my support—for now I meanT' unbosom to thee free without restraint:Search all the deep recesses of my soul,And open ev'ry darling thought before thee,Which long I've secreted with jealous care.Pray, mark me well.

VARDANES.

I will, my Royal Sire.

KING.

On Anna thus reclin'd the love-sick Dido;Thus to her cheek laid hers with gentle pressure,And wet her sister with a pearly show'r,Which fell from her sad eyes, then told her tale,While gentle Anna gave a pitying tear,And own'd 'twas moving—thou canst pity too,I know thy nature tender and engaging.

VARDANES.

Tell me, my gracious Lord, what moves you thus?Why is your breast distracted with these tumults?Teach me some method how to sooth your sorrows,And give your heart its former peace and joy;Instruct thy lov'd Vardanes.—

KING.

Yes, I'll tell thee;But listen with attention while I speak;And yet I know 'twill shock thy gentle soul,And horror o'er thee 'll spread his palsy hand.O, my lov'd Son! thou fondness of my age!Thou art the prop of my declining years,In thee alone I find a Father's joy,Of all my offspring: but Arsaces—

VARDANES.

Ha!My Brother!—

KING.

Ay—why dost start?—thy BrotherPursues me with his hate: and, while warm lifeRolls the red current thro' my veins, delightsTo see me tortur'd; with an easy smileHe meets my suff'rings, and derides my pain.

VARDANES.

Oh!

KING.

What means that hollow groan?—Vardanes, speak,Death's image fits upon thy pallid cheek,While thy low voice sounds as when murmurs runThro' lengthen'd vaults—

VARDANES.

O! my foreboding thoughts.

[*Aside.*

'Twas this disturb'd my rest; when sleep at nightLock'd me in slumbers; in my dreams I sawMy Brother's crime—yet, death!—it cannot be—

KING.

Ha!—what was that?—

VARDANES.

O! my dread Lord, some VillainBred up in lies, and train'd to treach'ry,Has injur'd you by vile reports, to stainMy Princely Brother's honour.

KING.

Thou know'st more,Thy looks confess what thou in vain wouldst hide—And hast thou then conspir'd against me too,And sworn concealment to your practices?—Thy guilt—

VARDANES.

Ha! guilt!—what guilt?—

KING.

Nay, start not so—I'll know your purposes, spite of thy art.

VARDANES.

O! ye great Gods! and is it come to this?—My Royal Father call your reason home,Drive these loud passions hence, that thus deform you.My Brother—Ah! what shall I say?—My BrotherSure loves you as he ought.

KING.

Ha! as he ought?—Hell blister thy evasive tongue—I'll know it—I will; I'll search thy breast, thus will I openA passage to your secrets—yet resolv'd—Yet steady in your horrid villany—'Tis fit that I from whom such monsters sprungNo more should burthen earth—Ye Parricides!—Here plant your daggers in this hated bosom—Here rive my heart, and end at once my sorrows,I gave ye being, that's the mighty crime.

VARDANES.

I can no more—here let me bow in anguish—Think not that I e'er join'd in his designs,Because I have conceal'd my knowledge of them:I meant, by pow'rful reason's friendly aid,To turn him from destruction's dreadful path,And bring him to a sense of what he ow'dTo you as King and Father.

KING.

Say on—I'll hear.

VARDANES.

He views thy sacred life with envious hate,As 'tis a bar to his ambitious hopes.On the bright throne of Empire his plum'd wishesSeat him, while on his proud aspiring browsHe feels the pleasing weight of Royalty.But when he wakes from these his airy dreams(Delusions form'd by the deceiver hope,To raise him to the glorious height of greatness),Then hurl him from proud Empire to subjection.Wild wrath will quickly swell his haughty breast,Soon as he finds 'tis but a shadowy blessing.—'Twas fav'ring accident discover'd to meAll that I know; this Evening as I stoodAlone, retir'd, in the still gallery,That leads up to th' appartment of my Brother,T' indulge my melancholy thoughts,—

KING.

Proceed—

VARDANES.

A wretch approach'd with wary step, his eyeSpoke half his tale, denoting villany.In hollow murmurs thus he question'd me—Was I the Prince?—I answer'd to content him—Then in his hand he held this paper forth."Take this," says he, "this Bethas greets thee with,Keep but your word our plot will meet success."I snatch'd it with more rashness than discretion,Which taught him his mistake. In haste he drew,And aim'd his dagger at my breast, but paidHis life, a forfeit, for his bold presuming.

KING.

O Villain! Villain!

VARDANES.

Here, read this, my Lord—I read it, and cold horror froze my blood.And shook me like an ague.

KING.

Ha!—what's this?—"Doubt not Arabia's aid, set me but free,I'll easy pass on the old cred'lous King,For fair Evanthe's Father."—Thus to atoms—Oh! could I tear these cursed traitors thus.

[*Tears the paper into pieces.*

VARDANES.

Curses avail you nothing, he has pow'r,And may abuse it to your prejudice.

KING.

I am resolv'd—

VARDANES.

Tho' Pris'ner in his camp,Yet, Bethas was attended like a Prince,As tho' he still commanded the Arabians.'Tis true, when they approach'd the royal city,He threw him into chains to blind our eyes,A shallow artifice—

KING.

That is a Truth.

VARDANES.

And, yet, he is your Son.

KING.

Ah! that indeed—

VARDANES.

Why, that still heightens his impiety,To rush to empire thro' his Father's blood,And, in return of life, to give him death.

KING.

Oh! I am all on fire, yes I must tearThese folds of venom from me.

VARDANES.

Sure 'twas LysiasThat cross'd the passage now.

KING.

'Tis to my wish.I'll in, and give him orders to arrestMy traitor Son and Bethas—Now VardanesIndulge thy Father in this one request—Seize, with some horse, Evanthe, and bear herTo your command—Oh! I'll own my weakness—I love with fondness mortal never knew—Not Jove himself, when he forsook his heav'n,And in a brutal shape disgrac'd the God,E'er lov'd like me.

VARDANES.

I will obey you, Sir.

SCENE IX.

VARDANES [*alone*].

I'll seize her, but I'll keep her for myself,It were a sin to give her to his age—To twine the blooming garland of the springAround the sapless trunks of wither'd oaks—The night, methinks, grows ruder than it was,Thus should it be, thus nature should be shock'd,And Prodigies, affrighting all mankind,Foretell the dreadful business I intend.The earth should gape, and swallow cities up,Shake from their haughty heights aspiring tow'rs,And level mountains with the vales below;The Sun amaz'd should frown in dark eclipse,And light retire to its unclouded heav'n;While darkness, bursting from her deep recess,Should wrap all nature in eternal night.—Ambition, glorious fever of the mind,'Tis that which raises us above mankind;The shining mark which bounteous heav'n has gave,From vulgar souls distinguishing the brave.

End of the Third Act.

ACT IV.

SCENE I. *A Prison.*

GOTARZES *and* PHRAATES.

PHRAATES.

Oh! fly my Prince, for safety dwells not here,Hence let me urge thy flight with eager haste.Last night thy Father sigh'd his soul to bliss,Base murther'd—

GOTARZES.

Murther'd? ye Gods!—

PHRAATES.

Alas! 'tis true.Stabb'd in his slumber by a traitor's hand;I scarce can speak it—horror choaks my words—Lysias it was who did the damned deed,Urg'd by the bloody Queen, and his curs'd rage,Because the King, thy Sire, in angry mood,Once struck him on his foul dishonest cheek.Suspicion gave me fears of this, when firstI heard, the Prince, Arsaces, was imprison'd,By fell Vardanes' wiles.

GOTARZES.

Oh! horror! horror!Hither I came to share my Brother's sorrows,To mingle tears, and give him sigh for sigh;But this is double, double weight of woe.

PHRAATES.

'Tis held as yet a secret from the world.Frighted by hideous dreams I shook off sleep,And as I mus'd the garden walks along,Thro' the deep gloom, close in a neighb'ring walk,Vardanes with proud Lysias I beheld,Still eager in discourse they saw not me,For yet the early dawn had not appear'd;I sought a secret stand, where hid from view,I heard stern Lysias, hail the Prince VardanesAs Parthia's dreaded Lord!—"'Tis done", he cry'd,"'Tis done, and Artabanus is no more.The blow he gave me is repay'd in blood;Now shall the morn behold two rising suns:Vardanes thou, our better light, shalt bringBright day and joy to ev'ry heart."

GOTARZES.

Why sleptYour vengeance, oh! ye righteous Gods?

PHRAATES.

Then toldA tale, so fill'd with bloody circumstance,Of this damn'd deed, that stiffen'd me with horror.Vardanes seem'd to blame the hasty act,As rash, and unadvis'd, by passion urg'd,Which never yields to cool reflection's place.But, being done, resolv'd it secret, lestThe multitude should take it in their wiseAuthority to pry into his death.Arsaces was, by assassination,Doom'd to fall. Your name was mention'd also—But hurried by my fears away, I leftThe rest unheard—

GOTARZES.

What can be done?—Reflection, why wilt thouForsake us, when distress is at our heels?Phraates, help me, aid me with thy council.

PHRAATES.

Then stay not here, fly to Barzaphernes,His conqu'ring troops are at a trivial distance;Soon will you reach the camp; he lov'd your Brother,And your Father with affection serv'd; hasteYour flight, whilst yet I have the city-guard,For Lysias I expect takes my command.I to the camp dispatch'd a trusty slave,Before the morn had spread her blushing veil.Away, you'll meet the Gen'ral on the road,On such a cause as this he'll not delay.

GOTARZES.

I thank your love—

SCENE II.

PHRAATES [*alone*].

I'll wait behind, my stayMay aid the cause; dissembling I must learn,Necessity shall teach me how to varyMy features to the looks of him I serve.I'll thrust myself disguis'd among the croud,And fill their ears with murmurs of the deed:Whisper all is not well, blow up the sparksOf discord, and it soon will flame to rage.

SCENE III.

QUEEN *and* LYSIAS.

QUEEN.

Haste, and shew me to the Prince Arsaces,Delay not, see the signet of Vardanes.

LYSIAS.

Royal Thermusa, why this eagerness?This tumult of the soul?—what means this dagger?Ha!—I suspect—

QUEEN.

Hold—for I'll tell thee, Lysias.'Tis—oh! I scarce can speak the mighty joy—I shall be greatly blest in dear revenge,'Tis vengeance on Arsaces—yes, this handShall urge the shining poniard to his heart,And give him death—yea, give the ruffian death;So shall I smile on his keen agonies.

LYSIAS.

Ha! am I robb'd of all my hopes of vengeance,Shall I then calmly stand with all my wrongs,And see another bear away revenge?

QUEEN.

For what can Lysias ask revenge, to barHis Queen of hers?

LYSIAS.

Was I not scorn'd, and spurn'd,With haughty insolence? like a base cowardRefus'd what e'er I ask'd, and call'd a boaster?My honour sullied, with opprobrious words,Which can no more its former brightness know,'Til, with his blood, I've wash'd the stains away.Say, shall I then not seek for glorious vengeance?

QUEEN.

And what is this, to the sad Mother's griefs,Her hope cut off, rais'd up with pain and care?Hadst thou e'er supported the lov'd Prattler?Hadst thou like me hung o'er his infancy,Wasting in wakeful mood the tedious night,And watch'd his sickly couch, far mov'd from rest,Waiting his health's return?—Ah! hadst thou knownThe parent's fondness, rapture, toil and sorrow,The joy his actions gave, and the fond wishOf something yet to come, to bless my age,And lead me down with pleasure to the grave,Thou wouldst not thus talk lightly of my wrongs.But I delay—

LYSIAS.

To thee I then submit.Be sure to wreck a double vengeance on him;If that thou knowst a part in all his body,Where pain can most be felt, strike, strike him there—And let him know the utmost height of anguish.It is a joy to think that he shall fall,Tho' 'tis another hand which gives the blow.

SCENE IV.

ARSACES *and* BETHAS.

ARSACES.

Why should I linger out my joyless days,When length of hope is length of misery?Hope is a coz'ner, and beguiles our cares,Cheats us with empty shews of happiness,Swift fleeting joys which mock the faint embrace;We wade thro' ills pursuing of the meteor,Yet are distanc'd still.

BETHAS.

Ah! talk not of hope—Hope fled when bright Astræa spurn'd this earth,And sought her seat among the shining Gods;Despair, proud tyrant, ravages my breast,And makes all desolation.

ARSACES.

How can IBehold those rev'rent sorrows, see those cheeksMoist with the dew which falls from thy sad eyes,Nor imitate distraction's frantic tricks,And chace cold lifeless reason from her throne?I am the fatal cause of all this sorrow,The spring of ills,—to know me is unhappiness;—And mis'ry, like a hateful plague, pursuesMy wearied steps, and blasts the springing verdure.

BETHAS.

No;—It is I that am the source of all,It is my fortune sinks you to this trouble;Before you shower'd your gentle pity on me,You shone the pride of this admiring world.—Evanthe springs from me, whose fatal charmsProduces all this ruin.—Hear me heav'n!If to another love she ever yields,And stains her soul with spotted falsehood's crime,If e'en in expectation tastes a bliss,Nor joins Arsaces with it, I will wreckMy vengeance on her, so that she shall beA dread example to all future times.

ARSACES.

Oh! curse her not, nor threaten her with anger,She is all gentleness, yet firm to truth,And blest with ev'ry pleasing virtue, freeFrom levity, her sex's character.She scorns to chace the turning of the wind,Varying from point to point.

BETHAS.

I love her, ye Gods!I need not speak the greatness of my love,Each look which straining draws my soul to hersDenotes unmeasur'd fondness; but mis'ry,Like a fretful peevish child, can scarce tellWhat it would wish, or aim at.

ARSACES.

Immortals, hear!Thus do I bow my soul in humble pray'r—Thou, King of beings, in whose breath is fate,Show'r on Evanthe all thy choicest blessings,And bless her with excess of happiness;If yet, there is one bliss reserv'd in store,And written to my name, oh! give it her,And give me all her sorrows in return.

BETHAS.

'Rise, 'rise my Prince, this goodness o'erwhelms me,She's too unworthy of so great a passion.

ARSACES.

I know not what it means, I'm not as usual,Ill-boding cares, and restless fears oppress me,And horrid dreams disturb, and fright, my slumbers;But yesternight, 'tis dreadful to relate,E'en now I tremble at my waking thoughts,Methought, I stood alone upon the shore,And, at my feet, there roll'd a sea of blood,High wrought, and 'midst the waves, appear'd my Father,Struggling for life; above him was Vardanes,Pois'd in the air, he seem'd to rule the storm,And, now and then, would push my Father down,And for a space he'd sink beneath the waves,And then, all gory, rise to open view,His voice in broken accents reach'd my ear,And bade me save him from the bloody stream;Thro' the red billows eagerly I rush'd,But sudden woke, benum'd with chilling fear.

BETHAS.

Most horrible indeed!—but let it pass,'Tis but the offspring of a mind disturb'd,For sorrow leaves impressions on the fancy,Which shew most fearful to us lock'd in sleep.

ARSACES.

Thermusa! ha!—what can be her design?She bears this way, and carries in her looksAn eagerness importing violence.Retire—for I would meet her rage alone.

SCENE V.

ARSACES *and* QUEEN.

ARSACES.

What means the proud Thermusa by this visit,Stoops heav'n-born pity to a breast like thine?Pity adorns th' virtuous, but ne'er dwellsWhere hate, revenge, and rage distract the soul.Sure, it is hate that hither urg'd thy steps,To view misfortune with an eye of triumph.I know thou lov'st me not, for I have dar'dTo cross thy purposes, and, bold in censure,Spoke of thy actions as they merited.Besides, this hand 'twas slew the curs'd Vonones.

QUEEN.

And darst thou insolent to name Vonones?To heap perdition on thy guilty soul?There needs not this to urge me to revenge—But let me view this wonder of mankind,Whose breath can set the bustling world in arms.I see no dreadful terrors in his eye,Nor gathers chilly fears around my heart,Nor strains my gazing eye with admiration,And, tho' a woman, I can strike the blow.

ARSACES.

Why gaze you on me thus? why hesitate?Am I to die?

QUEEN.

Thou art—this dagger shallDissolve thy life, thy fleeting ghost I'll sendTo wait Vonones in the shades below.

ARSACES.

And even there I'll triumph over him.

QUEEN.

O, thou vile homicide! thy fatal handHas robb'd me of all joy; Vonones, toThy Manes this proud sacrifice I give.That hand which sever'd the friendship of thySoul and body, shall never draw againImbitt'ring tears from sorr'wing mother's eyes.This, with the many tears I've shed, receive

[*Offers to stab him.*

Ha!—I'd strike; what holds my hand?—'tis n't pity.

ARSACES.

Nay, do not mock me, with the shew of death,And yet deny the blessing; I have metYour taunts with equal taunts, in hopes to urgeThe blow with swift revenge; but since that fails,I'll woo thee to compliance, teach my tonguePersuasion's winning arts, to gain thy soul;I'll praise thy clemency, in dying accentsBless thee for, this, thy charitable deed.Oh! do not stand; see, how my bosom heavesTo meet the stroke; in pity let me die,'Tis all the happiness I now can know.

QUEEN.

How sweet the eloquence of dying men!Hence Poets feign'd the music of the Swan,When death upon her lays his icy hand,She melts away in melancholy strains.

ARSACES.

Play not thus cruel with my poor request,But take my loving Father's thanks, and mine.

QUEEN.

Thy Father cannot thank me now.

ARSACES.

He will,Believe me, e'en whilst dissolv'd in ecstacyOn fond Evanthe's bosom, he will pause,One moment from his joys, to bless the deed.

QUEEN.

What means this tumult in my breast? from whenceProceeds this sudden change? my heart beats high,And soft compassion makes me less than woman:I'll search no more for what I fear to know.

ARSACES.

Why drops the dagger from thy trembling hand?Oh! yet be kind—

QUEEN.

No: now I'd have thee live,Since it is happiness to die: 'Tis painThat I would give thee, thus I bid thee live;Yes, I would have thee a whole age a dying,And smile to see thy ling'ring agonies.All day I'd watch thee, mark each heighten'd pang,While springing joy should swell my panting bosom;This I would have—But should this dagger giveThy soul the liberty it fondly wishes,'Twould soar aloft, and mock my faint revenge.

ARSACES.

This mildness shews most foul, thy anger lovely.Think that 'twas I who blasted thy fond hope,Vonones now lies number'd with the dead,And all your joys are buried in his grave;My hand untimely pluck'd the precious flow'r,Before its shining beauties were display'd.

QUEEN.

O Woman! Woman! where's thy resolution?Where's thy revenge? Where's all thy hopes of vengeance?Giv'n to the winds—Ha! is it pity?—No—I fear it wears another softer name.I'll think no more, but rush to my revenge,In spite of foolish fear, or woman's softness;Be steady now my soul to thy resolves.Yes, thou shalt die, thus, on thy breast, I writeThy instant doom—ha!—ye Gods!

[QUEEN *starts, as, in great fright, at hearing something.*

ARSACES.

Why this pause?Why dost thou idly stand like imag'd vengeance,With harmless terrors threatning on thy brow,With lifted arm, yet canst not strike the blow?

QUEEN.

It surely was the Echo to my fears,The whistling wind, perhaps, which mimick'd voice;But thrice methought it loudly cry'd, "Forbear."Imagination hence—I'll heed thee not—

[*Ghost of* ARTABANUS *rises.*

Save me—oh!—save me—ye eternal pow'rs!—See!—see it comes, surrounded with dread terrors—Hence—hence! nor blast me with that horrid sight—Throw off that shape, and search th' infernal roundsFor horrid forms, there's none can shock like thine.

GHOST.

No; I will ever wear this form, thus e'erAppear before thee; glare upon thee thus,'Til desperation, join'd to thy damn'd crime,Shall wind thee to the utmost height of frenzy.In vain you grasp the dagger in your hand,In vain you dress your brows in angry frowns,In vain you raise your threatning arm in air,Secure, Arsaces triumphs o'er your rage.Guarded by fate, from thy accurs'd revenge,Thou canst not touch his life; the Gods have giv'nA softness to thy more than savage soulBefore unknown, to aid their grand designs.Fate yet is lab'ring with some great event,But what must follow I'm forbid to broach—Think, think of me, I sink to rise again,To play in blood before thy aching sight,And shock thy guilty soul with hell-born horrors—Think, think of Artabanus! and despair—

[*Sinks.*

QUEEN.

Think of thee, and despair?—yes, I'll despair—Yet stay,—oh! stay, thou messenger of fate!Tell me—Ha! 'tis gone—and left me wretched—

ARSACES.

Your eyes seem fix'd upon some dreadful object,Horror and anguish clothe your whiten'd face,And your frame shakes with terror; I hear you speakAs seeming earnest in discourse, yet hearNo second voice.

QUEEN.

What! saw'st thou nothing?

ARSACES.

Nothing.

QUEEN.

Nor hear'd?—

ARSACES.

Nor Hear'd.

QUEEN.

Amazing spectacle!—Cold moist'ning dews distil from ev'ry pore,I tremble like to palsied age—Ye Gods!Would I could leave this loath'd detested being!—Oh! all my brain's on fire—I rave! I rave!—

[*Ghost rises again.*

Ha! it comes again—see, it glides along—See, see, what streams of blood flow from its wounds!A crimson torrent—Shield me, oh! shield me, heav'n.—

ARSACES.

Great, and righteous Gods!—

QUEEN.

Ah! frown not on me—Why dost thou shake thy horrid locks at me?Can I give immortality?—'tis gone—

[*Ghost sinks.*

It flies me, see, ah!—stop it, stop it, haste—

ARSACES.

Oh, piteous sight!—

QUEEN.

Hist! prithee, hist! oh death!I'm all on fire—now freezing bolts of iceDart thro' my breast—Oh! burst ye cords of life—Ha! who are ye?—Why do ye stare upon me?—Oh!—defend me, from these bick'ring Furies!

ARSACES.

Alas! her sense is lost, distressful Queen!

QUEEN.

Help me, thou King of Gods! oh! help me! help!—See! they envir'n me round—Vonones too,The foremost leading on the dreadful troop—But there, Vardanes beck'ns me to shunTheir hellish rage—I come, I come!Ah! they pursue me, with a scourge of fire.—

[*Runs out distracted.*

SCENE VI.

ARSACES [*alone*].

Oh!—horror!—on the ground she breathless lies,Silent, in death's cold sleep; the wall besmear'dWith brains and gore, the marks of her despair.O guilt! how dreadful dost thou ever shew!How lovely are the charms of innocence!How beauteous tho' in sorrows and distress!—Ha!—what noise?—

[*Clashing of swords.*

SCENE VII.

ARSACES, BARZAPHERNES *and* GOTARZES.

BARZAPHERNES.

At length we've forc'd our entrance—O my lov'd Prince! to see thee thus, indeed,Melts e'en me to a woman's softness; seeMy eyes o'erflow—Are these the ornamentsFor Royal hands? rude manacles! oh shameful!Is this thy room of state, this gloomy goal?Without attendance, and thy bed the pavement?But, ah! how diff'rent was our parting last!When flush'd with vict'ry, reeking from the slaughter,You saw Arabia's Sons scour o'er the plainIn shameful flight, before your conqu'ring sword;Then shone you like the God of battle.

ARSACES.

Welcome!Welcome, my loyal friends! Barzaphernes!My good old soldier, to my bosom thus!Gotarzes, my lov'd Brother! now I'm happy.—But, say, my soldier, why these threatning arms?Why am I thus releas'd by force? my Father,I should have said the King, had he relented,He'd not have us'd this method to enlarge me.Alas! I fear, too forward in your love,You'll brand me with the rebel's hated name.

BARZAPHERNES.

I am by nature blunt—the soldier's manner.Unus'd to the soft arts practis'd at courts.Nor can I move the passions, or disguiseThe sorr'wing tale to mitigate the smart.Then seek it not: I would sound the alarm,Loud as the trumpet's clangour, in your ears;Nor win I hail you, as our Parthia's King,'Til you've full reveng'd your Father's murther.

ARSACES.

Murther?—good heav'n!

BARZAPHERNES.

The tale requires some time;And opportunity must not be lost;Your traitor Brother, who usurps your rights,Must, ere his faction gathers to a head,Have from his brows his new-born honours torn.

ARSACES.

What, dost thou say, murther'd by Vardanes?Impious parricide!—detested villain!—Give me a sword, and onward to the charge,Stop gushing tears, for I will weep in blood,And sorrow with the groans of dying men.—Revenge! revenge!—oh!—all my soul's on fire!

GOTARZES.

'Twas not Vardanes struck the fatal blow,Though, great in pow'r usurp'd, he dares supportThe actor, vengeful Lysias; to his breastHe clasps, with grateful joy, the bloody villain;Who soon meant, with ruffian wiles, to cutYou from the earth, and also me.

ARSACES.

Just heav'ns!—But, gentle Brother, how didst thou eludeThe vigilant, suspicious, tyrant's craft?

GOTARZES.

Phraates, by an accident, obtain'dThe knowledge of the deed, and warn'd by himI bent my flight toward the camp, to seekProtection and revenge; but scarce I'd leftThe city when I o'ertook the Gen'ral.

BARZAPHERNES.

Ere the sun 'rose I gain'd th' intelligence:The soldiers when they heard the dreadful tale,First stood aghast, and motionless with horror.Then suddenly, inspir'd with noble rage,Tore up their ensigns, calling on their leadersTo march them to the city instantly.I, with some trusty few, with speed came forward,To raise our friends within, and gain your freedom.Nor hazard longer, by delays, your safety.Already faithful Phraates has gain'dA num'rous party of the citizens;With these we mean t' attack the Royal Palace,Crush the bold tyrant with surprise, while sunkIn false security; and vengeance wreck,Ere that he thinks the impious crime be known.

ARSACES.

O! parent being, Ruler of yon heav'n!Who bade creation spring to order, hear me.What ever sins are laid upon my soul,Now let them not prove heavy on this day,To sink my arm, or violate my cause.The sacred rights of Kings, my Country's wrongs,The punishment of fierce impiety,And a lov'd Father's death, call forth my sword.—

Now on; I feel all calm within my breast,And ev'ry busy doubt is hush'd to rest;Smile heav'n propitious on my virtuous cause,Nor aid the wretch who dares disdain your laws.

End of the Fourth Act.

ACT V.

SCENE I. *The Palace.*

The Curtain rises, slowly, to soft music, and discovers EVANTHE *sleeping on a sofa; after the music ceases,* VARDANES *enters.*

VARDANES.

Now shining Empire standing at the goal,Beck'ns me forward to increase my speed;But, yet, Arsaces lives, bane to my hopes,Lysias I'll urge to ease me of his life,Then give the villain up to punishment.The shew of justice gains the changeling croud,Besides, I ne'er will harbour in my bosomSuch serpents, ever ready with their stings—But now one hour for love and fair

Evanthe—Hence with ambition's cares—see, where reclin'd,In slumbers all her sorrows are dismiss'd,Sleep seems to heighten ev'ry beauteous feature,And adds peculiar softness to each grace.She weeps—in dreams some lively sorrow pains her—I'll take one kiss—oh! what a balmy sweetness!Give me another—and another still—For ever thus I'd dwell upon her lips.Be still my heart, and calm unruly transports.—Wake her, with music, from this mimic death.

[*Music sounds.*

SONG.

Tell me, Phillis, tell me why,You appear so wond'rous coy,When that glow, and sparkling eye,Speak you want to taste the joy?Prithee, give this fooling o'er,Nor torment your lover more.

While youth is warm within our veins,And nature tempts us to be gay,Give to pleasure loose the reins,Love and youth fly swift away.Youth in pleasure should be spent,Age will come, we'll then repent.

EVANTHE [*waking*].

I come, ye lovely shades—Ha! am I here?Still in the tyrant's palace? Ye bright pow'rs!Are all my blessings then but vis'onary?Methought I was arriv'd on that blest shoreWhere happy souls for ever dwell, crown'd withImmortal bliss; Arsaces led me throughThe flow'ry groves, while all around me gleam'dThousand and thousand shades, who welcom'd meWith pleasing songs of joy—Vardanes, ha!—

VARDANES.

Why beams the angry lightning of thine eyeAgainst thy sighing slave? Is love a crime?Oh! if to dote, with such excess of passionAs rises e'en to mad extravaganceIs criminal, I then am so, indeed.

EVANTHE.

Away! vile man!—

VARDANES.

If to pursue thee e'erWith all the humblest offices of love,If ne'er to know one single thought that doesNot bear thy bright idea, merits scorn—

EVANTHE.

Hence from my sight—nor let me, thus, polluteMine eyes, with looking on a wretch like thee,Thou cause of all my ills; I sicken atThy loathsome presence—

VARDANES.

'Tis not always thus,Nor dost thou ever meet the sounds of loveWith rage and fierce disdain: Arsaces, soon,Could smooth thy brow, and melt thy icy breast.

EVANTHE.

Ha! does it gall thee? Yes, he could, he could;Oh! when he speaks, such sweetness dwells uponHis accents, all my soul dissolves to love,And warm desire; such truth and beauty join'd!His looks are soft and kind, such gentlenessSuch virtue swells his bosom! in his eyeSits majesty, commanding ev'ry heart.Strait as the pine, the pride of all the grove,More blooming than the spring, and sweeter far,Than asphodels or roses infant sweets.Oh! I could dwell forever on his praise,Yet think eternity was scarce enoughTo tell the mighty theme; here in my breastHis image dwells, but one dear thought of him,When fancy paints his Person to my eye,As he was wont in tenderness dissolv'd,Sighing his vows, or kneeling at my feet,Wipes off all mem'ry of my wretchedness.

VARDANES.

I know this brav'ry is affected, yetIt gives me joy, to think my rival onlyCan in imagination taste thy beauties.Let him,—'twill ease him in his solitude,And gild the horrors of his prison-house,Till death shall—

EVANTHE.

Ha! what was that? till death—ye Gods!Ah, now I feel distress's tort'ring pang—Thou canst not, villain—darst not think his death—O mis'ry!—

VARDANES.

Naught but your kindness saves him,Yet bless me, with your love, and he is safe;But the same frown which kills my growing hopes,Gives him to death.

EVANTHE.

O horror, I could dieTen thousand times to save the lov'd Arsaces.Teach me the means, ye pow'rs, how to save him:Then lead me to what ever is my fate.

VARDANES.

Not only shall he die, but to thy viewI'll bring the scene, those eyes that take delightIn cruelty, shall have enough of death.E'en here, before thy sight, he shall expire,Not sudden, but by ling'ring torments; allThat mischief can invent shall be practis'dTo give him pain; to lengthen out his woeI'll search around the realm for skillful men,To find new tortures.

EVANTHE.

Oh! wrack not thus my soul!

VARDANES.

The sex o'erflows with various humours, heWho catches not their smiles the very moment,Will lose the blessing—I'll improve this softness.—

[*Aside to her.*

Heav'n never made thy beauties to destroy,They were to bless, and not to blast mankind;Pity should dwell within thy lovely breast,That sacred temple ne'er was form'd for hateA habitation; but a residenceFor love and gaiety.

EVANTHE.

Oh! heav'ns!

VARDANES.

That sigh,Proclaims your kind consent to save Arsaces.

[*Laying hold of her.*

EVANTHE.

Ha! villain, off—unhand me—hence—

VARDANES.

In vainIs opportunity to those, who spendAn idle courtship on the fair, they wellDeserve their fate, if they're disdain'd;—her charmsTo rush upon, and conquer opposition,Gains the Fair one's praise; an active loverSuits, who lies aside the coxcomb's empty whine,And forces her to bliss.

EVANTHE.

Ah! hear me, hear me,Thus kneeling, with my tears, I do implore thee:Think on my innocence, nor force a joyWhich will ever fill thy soul with anguish.Seek not to load my ills with infamy,Let me not be a mark for bitter scorn,To bear proud virtue's taunts and mocking jeers,And like a flow'r, of all its sweetness robb'd,Be trod to earth, neglected and disdain'd,And spurn'd by ev'ry vulgar saucy foot.

VARDANES.

Speak, speak forever—music's in thy voice,Still attentive will I listen to thee,Be hush'd as night, charm'd with the magic sound.

EVANTHE.

Oh! teach me, heav'n, soft moving eloquence,To bend his stubborn soul to gentleness.—Where is thy virtue? Where thy princely lustre?Ah! wilt thou meanly stoop to do a wrong,And stain thy honour with so foul a blot?Thou who shouldst be a guard to innocence.Leave force to brutes—for pleasure is not foundWhere still the soul's averse; horror and guilt,Distraction, desperation chace her hence.Some happier gentle Fair one you may find,Whose yielding heart may bend to meet your flame,In mutual love soft joys alone are found;When souls are drawn by secret sympathy,And virtue does on virtue smile.

VARDANES.

No more—Her heav'nly tongue will charm me from th' intent—Hence coward softness, force shall make me blest.

EVANTHE.

Assist me, ye bless't pow'rs!—oh! strike, ye Gods!Strike me, with thunder dead, this moment, e'erI suffer violation—

VARDANES.

'Tis in vain,The idle pray'rs by fancy'd grief put up,Are blown by active winds regardless by,Nor ever reach the heav'ns.

SCENE II.

VARDANES, EVANTHE *and* LYSIAS.

LYSIAS.

Arm, arm, my Lord!—

VARDANES.

Damnation! why this interruption now?—

LYSIAS.

Oh! arm! my noble Prince, the foe's upon us.Arsaces, by Barzaphernes releas'd,Join'd with the citizens, assaults the Palace,And swears revenge for Artabanus' death.

VARDANES.

Ha! what? revenge for Artabanus' death?—'Tis the curse of Princes that their counsels,Which should be kept like holy mysteries,Can never rest in silent secrecy.Fond of employ, some cursed tattling tongueWill still divulge them.

LYSIAS.

Sure some fiend from hell,In mischief eminent, to cross our views,Has giv'n th' intelligence, for man could not.

EVANTHE.

Oh! ever blest event!—All-gracious heav'n!This beam of joy revives me.

SCENE III.

VARDANES, EVANTHE, LYSIAS, *to them, an* OFFICER.

OFFICER.

Haste! my Lord!Or all will soon be lost; tho' thrice repuls'dBy your e'erfaithful guards, they still returnWith double fury.

VARDANES.

Hence, then, idle love—Come forth, my trusty sword—curs'd misfortune!—Had I but one short hour, without reluctance,I'd meet them, tho' they brib'd the pow'rs of hell,To place their furies in the van: Yea, rushTo meet this dreadful Brother 'midst the war—Haste to the combat—Now a crown or death—The wretch who dares to give an inch of groundTill I retire, shall meet the death he shun'd.Away—away! delays are dang'rous now—

SCENE IV.

EVANTHE [*alone*].

Now heav'n be partial to Arsaces' cause,Nor leave to giddy chance when virtue strives;Let victory sit on his warlike helm,For justice draws his sword: be thou his aid,And let the opposer's arm sink with the weightOf his most impious crimes—be still my heart,For all that thou canst aid him with is pray'r.Oh! that I had the strength of thousands in me!Or that my voice could wake the sons of menTo join, and crush the tyrant!—

SCENE V.

EVANTHE *and* CLEONE.

EVANTHE.

My Cleone—Welcome thou partner of my joys and sorrows.

CLEONE.

Oh! yonder terror triumphs uncontroul'd,And glutton death seems never satisfy'd.Each soft sensation lost in thoughtless rage,And breast to breast, oppos'd in furious war,The fiery Chiefs receive the vengeful steel.O'er lifeless heaps of men the soldiers climbStill eager for the combat, while the groundMade slipp'ry by the gushing streams of goreIs treach'rous to their feet.—Oh! horrid sight!—Too much for me to stand, my life was chill'd,As from the turret I beheld the fight,It forc'd me to retire.

EVANTHE.

What of Arsaces?

CLEONE.

I saw him active in the battle, now,Like light'ning, piercing thro' the thickest foe,Then scorning to disgrace his sword in lowPlebeian blood—loud for Vardanes call'd—To meet him singly, and decide the war.

EVANTHE.

Save him, ye Gods!—oh! all my soul is fear—Fly, fly Cleone, to the tow'r again,See how fate turns the ballance; and pursueArsaces with thine eye; mark ev'ry blow,Observe if some bold villain dares to urgeHis sword presumptuous at my Hero's breast.Haste, my Cleone, haste, to ease my fears.

SCENE VI.

EVANTHE [*alone*].

Ah!—what a cruel torment is suspense!My anxious soul is torn 'twixt love and fear,Scarce can I please me with one fancied blissWhich kind imagination forms, but reason,Proud, surly reason, snatches the vain joy,And gives me up again to sad distress.Yet I can die, and should Arsaces fallThis fatal draught shall ease me of my sorrows.

SCENE VII.

CLEONE [*alone*].

Oh! horror! horror! horror!—cruel Gods!—I saw him fall—I did—pierc'd thro' with wounds—Curs'd! curs'd Vardanes!—hear'd the gen'ral cry,Which burst, as tho' all nature had dissolv'd.Hark! how they shout! the noise seems coming this way.

SCENE VIII.

ARSACES, GOTARZES, BARZAPHERNES *and* OFFICERS, *with* VARDANES *and* LYSIAS, *prisoners.*

ARSACES.

Thanks to the ruling pow'rs who blest our arms,Prepare the sacrifices to the Gods,And grateful songs of tributary praise.—Gotarzes, fly, my Brother, find Evanthe,And bring the lovely mourner to my arms.

GOTARZES.

Yes, I'll obey you, with a willing speed.

[*Exit* GOTARZES.

ARSACES.

Thou, Lysias, from yon tow'r's aspiring heightBe hurl'd to death, thy impious hands are stain'dWith royal blood—Let the traitor's bodyBe giv'n to hungry dogs.

LYSIAS.

Welcome, grim death!—I've fed thy maw with Kings, and lack no moreRevenge—Now, do thy duty, Officer.

OFFICER.

Yea, and would lead all traitors gladly thus,—The boon of their deserts.

SCENE IX.

ARSACES, VARDANES, BARZAPHERNES.

ARSACES.

But for Vardanes,The Brother's name forgot—

VARDANES.

You need no more,I know the rest—Ah! death is near, my woundsPermit me not to live—my breath grows short,Curs'd be Phraates' arm which stop'd my sword,Ere it had reach'd thy proud exulting heart.But the wretch paid dear for his presuming;A just reward.—

ARSACES.

He sinks, yet bear him up—

VARDANES.

Curs'd be the multitude which o'erpow'r'd me,And beat me to the ground, cover'd with wounds—But, oh! 'tis done! my ebbing life is done—I feel death's hand upon me—Yet, I dieJust as I wish, and daring for a crown,Life without rule is my disdain; I scornTo swell a haughty Brother's sneaking train,To wait upon his ear with flatt'ring tales,And court his smiles; come, death, in thy cold arms,Let me forget Ambition's mighty toil,And shun the triumphs of a hated Brother—O! bear me off—Let not his eyes enjoyMy agonies—My sight grows dim with death.

[*They bear him off.*

SCENE (*the Last*).

ARSACES, GOTARZES, BARZAPHERNES, *and* EVANTHE *supported.*

EVANTHE.

Lead me, oh! lead me, to my lov'd Arsaces.Where is he?—

ARSACES.

Ha! what's this?—Just heav'ns!—my fears—

EVANTHE.

Arsaces, oh! thus circl'd in thy arms,I die without a pang.

ARSACES.

Ha! die?—why stare ye,Ye lifeless ghosts? Have none of ye a tongueTo tell me I'm undone?

GOTARZES.

Soon, my Brother,Too soon, you'll know it by the sad effects;And if my grief will yet permit my tongueTo do its office, thou shalt hear the tale.Cleone, from the turret, view'd the battle,And on Phraates fix'd her erring sight,Thy brave unhappy friend she took for thee,By his garb deceiv'd, which like to thine he wore.Still with her eye she follow'd him, where e'erHe pierc'd the foe, and to Vardanes' swordShe saw him fall a hapless victim, then,In agonies of grief, flew to Evanthe,And told the dreadful tale—the fatal bowlI saw—

ARSACES.

Be dumb, nor ever give againFear to the heart, with thy ill-boding voice.

EVANTHE.

Here, I'll rest, till death, on thy lov'd bosom,Here let me sigh my—Oh! the poison works—

ARSACES.

Oh! horror!—

EVANTHE.

Cease—this sorrow pains me moreThan all the wringing agonies of death,The dreadful parting of the soul from, this,Its wedded clay—Ah! there—that pang shot thro'My throbbing heart—

ARSACES.

Save her, ye Gods!—oh! save her!And I will bribe ye with clouds of incense;Such num'rous sacrifices, that your altarsShall even sink beneath the mighty load.

EVANTHE.

When I am dead, dissolv'd to native dust,Yet let me live in thy dear mem'ry—One tear will not be much to give Evanthe.

ARSACES.

My eyes shall e'er two running fountains be,And wet thy urn with overflowing tears,Joy ne'er again within my breast shall findA residence—Oh! speak, once more—

EVANTHE.

Life's just out—My Father—Oh! protect his honour'd age,And give him shelter from the storms of fate,He's long been fortune's sport—Support me—Ah!—I can no more—my glass is spent—farewell—Forever—Arsaces!—Oh!

[*Dies.*

ARSACES.

Stay, oh! stay,Or take me with thee—dead! she's cold and dead!Her eyes are clos'd, and all my joys are flown—Now burst ye elements, from your restraint,Let order cease, and chaos be again.Break! break, tough heart!—

oh! torture—life dissolve—Why stand ye idle? Have I not one friendTo kindly free me from this pain? One blow,One friendly blow would give me ease.

BARZAPHERNES.

The GodsForefend!—Pardon me, Royal Sir, if IDare, seemingly disloyal, seize your sword,Despair may urge you far—

ARSACES.

Ha! traitors! rebels!—Hoary rev'rend Villain! what, disarm me?Give me my sword—what, stand ye by, and seeYour Prince insulted? Are ye rebels all?—

BARZAPHERNES.

Be calm, my gracious Lord!

GOTARZES.

Oh! my lov'd Brother!

ARSACES.

Gotarzes too! all! all! conspir'd against me?Still, are ye all resolv'd that I must live,And feel the momentary pangs of death?—Ha!—this, shall make a passage for my soul—

[*Snatches* BARZAPHERNES' *sword.*

Out, out vile cares, from your distress'd abode—

[*Stabs himself.*

BARZAPHERNES.

Oh! ye eternal Gods!

GOTARZES.

Distraction! heav'ns!I shall run mad—

ARSACES.

Ah! 'tis in vain to grieve—The steel has done its part, and I'm at rest.—Gotarzes, wear my crown, and be thou blest,Cherish, Barzaphernes, my trusty chief—I faint, oh! lay me by Evanthe's side—Still wedded in our deaths—Bethas—

BARZAPHERNES.

Despair,My Lord, has broke his heart, I saw him stretch'd,Along the flinty pavement, in his gaol—Cold, lifeless—

ARSACES.

He's happy then—had he heardThis tale, he'd—Ah! Evanthe chides my soul,For ling'ring here so long—another pangAnd all the world, adieu—oh! adieu!—

[*Dies.*

GOTARZES.

Oh!Fix me, heav'n, immoveable, a statue,And free me from o'erwhelming tides of grief.

BARZAPHERNES.

Oh! my lov'd Prince, I soon shall follow thee;Thy laurel'd glories whither are they fled?—Would I had died before this fatal day!—Triumphant garlands pride my soul no more,No more the lofty voice of war can charm—And why then am I here? Thus then—

[*Offers to stab himself.*

GOTARZES.

Ah! hold,Nor rashly urge the blow—think of me, andLive—My heart is wrung with streaming anguish,Tore with the smarting pangs of woe, yet, will IDare to live, and stem misfortune's billows.Live then, and be the guardian of my youth,And lead me on thro' virtue's rugged path.

BARZAPHERNES.

O, glorious youth, thy words have rous'd theDrooping genius of my soul; thus, let meClasp thee, in my aged arms; yes, I will live—Live, to support thee in thy kingly rights,And when thou 'rt firmly fix'd, my task's perform'd,My honourable task—Then I'll retire,Petition gracious heav'n to bless my work,And in the silent grave forget my cares.

GOTARZES.

Now, to the Temple, let us onward move,And strive t' appease the angry pow'rs above.Fate yet may have some ills reserv'd in store,Continu'd curses, to torment us more.Tho', in their district, Monarchs rule alone,Jove sways the mighty Monarch on his throne:Nor can the shining honours which they wear,Purchase one joy, or save them from one care.

Finis.

FOOTNOTES:

[5] The Tigris.

Milton Keynes UK
Ingram Content Group UK Ltd.
UKHW030626061024
449204UK00004B/278

9 789362 090058